PASCAL
PROGRA

P RADHA GANESHAN

Programmer
Thiagarajar College
Madurai

Publishing Globally

NEW AGE INTERNATIONAL (P) LIMITED, PUBLISHERS
LONDON • NEW DELHI • NAIROBI
Bangalore • Chennai • Cochin • Guwahati • Hyderabad • Kolkata • Lucknow • Mumbai
Visit us at **www.newagepublishers.com**

GLOBAL OFFICES

- **New Delhi** NEW AGE INTERNATIONAL (P) LIMITED, PUBLISHERS
  7/30 A, Daryaganj, New Delhi-110002, (INDIA)
  Tel.: (011) 23253771, 23253472, **Telefax:** 23267437, 43551305
  E-mail: contactus@newagepublishers.com • Visit us at www.newagepublishers.com

- **London** NEW AGE INTERNATIONAL (UK) LTD.
  27 Old Gloucester Street, London, WC1N 3AX, UK
  E-mail: info@newacademicscience.co.uk • Visit us at www.newacademicscience.co.uk

- **Nairobi** NEW AGE GOLDEN (EAST AFRICA) LTD.
  Ground Floor, Westlands Arcade, Chiromo Road (Next to Naivas Supermarket)
  Westlands, Nairobi, KENYA, **Tel.:** 00-254-713848772, 00-254-725700286
  E-mail: kenya@newagepublishers.com

BRANCHES

- **Bangalore** 37/10, 8th Cross (Near Hanuman Temple), Azad Nagar, Chamarajpet, Bangalore- 560 018
  Tel.: (080) 26756823, **Telefax:** 26756820, **E-mail: bangalore@newagepublishers.com**

- **Chennai** 26, Damodaran Street, T. Nagar, Chennai-600 017, **Tel.:** (044) 24353401
  Telefax: 24351463, **E-mail: chennai@newagepublishers.com**

- **Cochin** CC-39/1016, Carrier Station Road, Ernakulam South, Cochin-682 016
  Tel.: (0484) 2377303, **Telefax:** 4051304, **E-mail: cochin@newagepublishers.com**

- **Guwahati** Hemsen Complex, Mohd. Shah Road, Paltan Bazar, Near Starline Hotel
  Guwahati-781 008, **Tel.:** (0361) 2513881, **Telefax:** 2543669
  E-mail: guwahati@newagepublishers.com

- **Hyderabad** 105, 1st Floor, Madhiray Kaveri Tower, 3-2-19, Azam Jahi Road, Near Kumar Theater
  Nimboliadda Kachiguda, Hyderabad-500 027, **Tel.:** (040) 24652456, **Telefax:** 24652457
  E-mail: hyderabad@newagepublishers.com

- **Kolkata** RDB Chambers (Formerly Lotus Cinema) 106A, 1st Floor, S N Banerjee Road
  Kolkata-700 014, **Tel.:** (033) 22273773, **Telefax:** 22275247
  E-mail: kolkata@newagepublishers.com

- **Lucknow** 16-A, Jopling Road, Lucknow-226 001, **Tel.:** (0522) 2209578, 4045297, **Telefax:** 220406
  E-mail: lucknow@newagepublishers.com

- **Mumbai** 142C, Victor House, Ground Floor, N.M. Joshi Marg, Lower Parel, Mumbai-400 013
  Tel.: (022) 24927869, **Telefax:** 24915415, **E-mail: mumbai@newagepublishers.com**

- **New Delhi** 22, Golden House, Daryaganj, New Delhi-110 002, **Tel.:** (011) 23262368, 23262370
  Telefax: 43551305, **E-mail: sales@newagepublishers.com**

ISBN: 978-81-224-1096-9

C-17-05-10441

Printed in India at Kanishik Printing Press, Delhi.

NEW AGE INTERNATIONAL (P) LIMITED, PUBLISHERS
7/30 A, Daryaganj, New Delhi-110002
Visit us at **www.newagepublishers.com**
(CIN: U74899DL1966PTC004618)

Dedicated to

**KALAITHANTHAI KARUMUTTU
THIAGARAJAN CHETTIAR**

AND

KALAIANNAI Dr. RADHA THIAGARAJAN

PREFACE

Computers are being used in the fast developing and competitive world to solve the problems quickly with plenty of available data. In the expanding field of computer education, one of the fastest growing, versatile and much sought after language is Pascal. Any one can understand the principles of this language with much ease if he thinks logically.

In this book, the concepts related to the syntax of the language are introduced. These concepts are explained in a systematic way with many examples for easy understanding by the readers.

Beginning with a simple introduction to Pascal, the book explains the fundamentals of the language in a simple and lucid style. This is followed by Control statements, Arrays, Procedures and Functions, Records, Files and Pointers. In each chapter a good number of solved problems are given to make the reader understand the tenets of Pascal. The reader is also inspired to delve into problem-solving, by the exercises given at the end of each chapter.

There are separate chapters on Graphics, and OOP (Object Oriented Programming) which give the reader an insight into fascinating program applications in Pascal. The programs given in the solved problems and exercises of this book have been tested on Turbo Pascal Version 5.5. In short, this book is a comprehensive Introduction to Pascal for Beginners.

P. Radha Ganeshan

Acknowledgements

I am thankful to several people for the assistance they rendered to me which made this book a reality. In particular I am indebted to Karumuttu T.Kannan, Correspondent, and Dr. S.Chockalingam, Principal of Thiagarajar College, Madurai who have encouraged me to write this book.

I place on record my sincere thanks to Dr. R.Murugesan, for inspiring me to write books on computer,

- Prof. M.Thangaraj, Prof. U.Jeyasudharsan, Prof. A.Kandaswamy, Prof. V.S.Meenakshi, Prof. M.Jabir Hussain, Miss J.Jeyanthi, Mr. P.Rajkumar and Miss R.Savithri for in-depth editing and manuscript enhancement.

- Mr. P.Srinivasan, Software Consultant whose editorial assistance was immensely responsible for the quality improvement of my work.

- Dr. E. Papavinasam, for the system support provided by him.

- Mr. J.Jeyasankar, Miss P.Jeyalakshmi, Miss R.Malathy, Mr. Ramalingam, Mrs. Surya Natraj and Mr. Karthi for software support provided by them.

- Miss B.Raja Rajeswari for helping me to get through the stressful times.

- The members of the faculty of Departments of Physics and Computer Science, Thiagarajar College for their encouragement given by them, then and there.

- Prof. V.T.Sadasivan and Prof.M.Palaniappan, Who have inspired me to write my first book on Computers.

- Prof. N.Thirunavukkarasu and Dr. M.Arunagirii for their valuable support at all times.

- Members of HERTZ family for their inspiring factor for my work.

- Dr. N.Srinivasan, Co-author of my previous book "C in 10 Hours" has provided useful hints for writing this book. I thank him heartily.

I owe my many thanks to M/s Venkatesh, Siva, Kishore, Rajan, Kalai, Pradeep, Prakash, Prem, Saravanan, Rajesh, Anbu, Siva, Jothi, Muthu, Jayanthi, Nagaraj and Raji for setting up an environment to write this book.

A number of my students have helped me by going through the proofs and giving useful suggestions. I thank them heartily.

Finally, I would like to thank all those who have not only supported, guided and helped me in this project, but also provided their feedback and criticism.

My special thanks to M/s New Age International (P) Ltd., Publishers for motivating me to write this book.

P. Radha Ganeshan

CONTENTS

LIST OF PASCAL PROGRAMS

CHAPTER - 1

INTRODUCTION

Three discoveries were supposed to be the greatest in human civilisation: Speech, Wheel and Electricity. As the twentieth century draws to a close, the maxim changes – there are four great discoveries. Needless to say, the fourth greatest discovery is Computer. Computer is like a servant. As the servant obeys our request, Computer obeys our orders. Orders are also called "Instructions" and a set of instruction is called a "Program".

To interact with Computers we need a medium through which Computers can understand. For that, we use computer languages. The language similar to our English language is called High Level Language. There are about 600 high level languages in the field. Some of them are obsolete and some of them are for specific purposes. Languages are classified as Scientific purpose languages, Commercial purpose languages and all purpose languages.

For Scientific Purposes we use FORTRAN (FORmula TRANslation). It was developed by a crew led by JOHN BACKUS in 1952–58 at the International Business Machine (IBM). It mostly finds its usefulness in Scientific problems. For commercial purposes we use COBOL (COmmon Business Oriented Language). Its presence in business organisation is vital because of its file handling facility. It was developed in a conference (CODASYL) attended by System programmers and Industrialists at Pentagon in early 1960's. Then there was a need for a language which satisfies both the ends, and it was fulfilled by JOHN KEMENY and THOMOS KURTZ who developed the BASIC (Beginners All Purpose Symbolic Instruction Code) at Dartmouth College, New Hampshire in 1964. The ease of this language made both the scientific and commercial areas flourishing.

Now one may raise his eyebrow as to why we learn PASCAL while we have BASIC already. The reasons for choosing PASCAL as our programming language are as follows.

STRUCTURED LANGUAGE

The program flow can be divided into three viz., sequential flow, selective flow and repetitive flow. Normally in other languages (BASIC and FORTRAN) we use goto statement to byepass a group of statements. The usage of goto is inevitable as there are no alternative statements available in these languages. But Pascal supports many looping and various forms of decision making statements and made us not to use goto in most of the circumstances. By using these statements one can write a structured program although there are no specific rules for it. The word "Structured" was coined by a famous algorithmist Dijkstra, who quoted in one of his papers as, "Goto should be completely abolished from all high level languages". In Pascal we may avoid GOTO in most of the situations. This not only enhances the program but also leads to a neat program flow. The language which uses goto abundantly is called 'Sphaghetti language' as shown in Fig. 1.1.

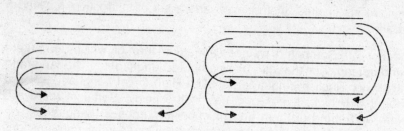

Fig. 1.1.

MODULARITY

It is also one of the special features that is not available in other languages when Pascal comes into the field. We can divide a very big program into many subprograms (or modules) which enable us to code and trace the program very easily. This feature also avoids the redundancy of coding and this feature is clearly explained in Chapter 6.

TEACHING LANGUAGE

We need a structured language to be taught at the graduate level, and PASCAL is the best choice. The easy flow of the language helps every one to write programs comfortably.

FUTURE LANGUAGE

PASCAL is considered as a Future language because of the growing demand for an all purpose language in the computer world. The programs written in those days by using non-structured languages such as BASIC and FORTRAN are rewritten by using PASCAL. Hence it becomes the choice of a new generation.

HISTORY OF PASCAL LANGUAGE

Like many languages PASCAL also originated from ALGOL-60. In 1970 a famous scientist and algorithmist Nikalus Wirth developed this wonderful language at the Technical University, Zurich, Switzerland. He developed this language to cater to the needs of both scientific and commercial demands. He wanted a suitable name for his language and to honour the scientist BLAISE PASCAL (One who developed the first Adding machine in 1642) he named his language as PASCAL. Initially the cost of the compiler was too high and one could not afford to buy it. Later when Borland International Inc.,entered into the market and marketed its TURBO PASCAL, suddenly the cost of the compiler came down from 500$ to 50$ and hence the language was picked up by all universities and research centres.

COMPILERS AVAILABLE FOR PASCAL

The program which is written by a programmer is called source program. But, computers understand only the machine language form, so it is necessary to use compilers to convert high level language to machine language and the converted program is called object program.

Of all the compilers available for PASCAL, quite few are widely used and accepted by the programmers. Turbo Pascal from Borland Inc., and Quick Pascal from Microsoft are to name a few.

CHAPTER - 2

FUNDAMENTALS OF PASCAL

As we have already seen high level languages are English like. They use the same alphabets of English. The characters set used by PASCAL language is given below.

Alphabets	:	A to Z, a to z
Numbers	:	0 – 9
Special characters	:	+ – * / , . ; = ^ [ ] { } ( ) > < '

Pascal is not a case sensitive language, and it takes AREA, Area, area to be one and the same.

STRUCTURE OF PASCAL

How can one differentiate pascal from other high level languages?. Only structure of a language can distinguish it from other languages. So, it is very important to understand the structure of Pascal before writing a program in it.

The prototype of a pascal program is given below.

```
PROGRAM Prog. Name (Input, Output);
label
Const
Type definition
Variables
Procedures
Function
{main starts}
Begin
   Statements;
End.
```

I. Header

Every product in this world has its own identity, why not our programs?, The header of the Pascal program looks like

```
PROGRAM  Prog.Name  (INPUT, QUTPUT);
```

PROGRAM is a reserved word supported by the language compiler, and Prog. Name is given by the user (i.e.Programmer). The rules for framing Prog. Name are as follows.

1. The first letter must be an alphabet.

2. The following letters may be either numbers or alphabets.

3. No special characters should be used including blank space.

4. Underscore may be used for better readability but it must be embedded.

5. The maximum length is 63 characters. (In case you exceed 63 characters PASCAL will consider only the first 63 characters)

INPUT, OUTPUT given within parentheses indicates that the program receives some input from the user and in return, it supplies some useful result to the user. The " ; " used here is for statement separator.

The following are some examples for header.

```
PROGRAM area (INPUT, OUTPUT);
PROGRAM AREA (OUTPUT, INPUT);
PROGRAM area ;
```

The header is optional in TURBO PASCAL and it is compulsory for some variants of PASCAL.

II. BLOCK

The block is divided into declaration part and statement part. In BASIC and FORTRAN there is no need to declare the variable used in it. Whereas a structured language like PASCAL expects all the variables used in the program to be declared before it executes any computation.

The declaration takes the following form.

a. Label

Even though GOTO should be avoided in many situations, there are some circumstances where GOTO is necessary for program clarity. Before using GOTO it should be declared in the Label part, and declaration of label is as follows.

LABEL
    100, 200 ;   •

The above statement indicates that there are two GOTO statements in the program and uses 100 and 200 as its label. Also note that labels may be alphanumeric, whereas other languages lack this facility. Here is an example which uses alphanur   a   abel.

LABEL

    para1, para2 ;

The readers are advised to avoid GOTO as far as possible since undue use of GOTO may lead to confusion.

b. Constant

It is defined as the value of a quantity which does not vary during the program execution. Suppose in one of our program we want to have dollar as a constant in many places, it is accomplished simply by defining it in the constant area.

CONST

    dollar = 31.50;

By making this definition, wherever dollar occurs in the program, it is assigned the value 31.50. The important note to the programmer is that, the value of a constant should not be varied in the program i.e. it is neither incremented nor decremented. Also it leads to error when an expression is used instead of a constant term. Let us see this through some definition.

An invalid constant definition

CONST

    PHI = 22/7 ;

A valid constant definition

CONST

    PHI = 3.1428 ;

c. Type Definition

Beside the standard types available in PASCAL, type definition allows the user to define their own data types. It will be discussed more elaborately in Chapter 6.

d. Variables

It is defined as the value of a quantity which varies during the program execution.

PASCAL supports the following variable types.

    Integer

Real

Char

Boolean

Let us see them one by one with examples.

Integer

Integer is the number without a fractional part. The rules to be followed while defining an integer are as follows.

i. Commas cannot appear anywhere in a number.

ii. Every number must be preceded by sign (+,–) and it is assumed to be positive if there is no sign.

iii. The Integer range is

–32768 to +32767

It occupies 2 bytes in Memory.

Valid Integer.	Invalid Integer.
1234	1,000
–7680	+–890
	654.89

Assume that we want to use a,b,c as integer variable in our program. Then the declaration takes the following form

VAR

a,b,c : integer ;

In addition to the above types the latest version of TURBO PASCAL provides few more types to facilitate the program. They are

Longint

i. The range is from –2147483648 to +2147483647.

ii. It occupies four bytes of memory.

Shortint

i. The range for this type is from –128 to +127.

ii. It occupies one byte of memory.

Byte

  i. The range is from 0 to 255 (unsigned shortint).

  ii. The memory required to store this type is same as shortint.

Word

  i. The range is from 0 to 65535 (unsigned integer).

  ii. The memory required to store this type is same as integer.

an example declaration is

> **VAR**
>
> > a : integer ;
> > b : longint ;
> > c : Word ;
> > d : Shortint ;
> > e : byte ;

Real

Numbers with fractional part are known as real. The rules for defining the real are same as those for integer.

Valid Real	Invalid Real
123,45	8,900.87
– 56.45	= – 844.65

The value .5 or 5. is valid in some languages whereas it is invalid in PASCAL. Here decimal point is always embedded.

So, .5 should be written as 0.5

and 5. should be written as 5.0

When considering storage, it occupies six bytes in memory with 11 digits of accuracy. For example, if we want to use x,y,z as real variables, then our declaration might look like

> **VAR**
>
> > x,y,z : real ;

Like integer which has few modifiers, real also has few more modifiers and it mainly depends on math co–processor.

Single

i. The range is from $1.5 * 10^{-45}$ to $3.4 * 10^{38}$.

ii. It occupies four bytes of memory with 7 or 8 digits of accuracy.

Double

i. The range is from $5.0 * 10^{-324}$ to $1.7 * 10^{308}$.

ii. It occupies eight bytes of memory and provides 15 or 16 digits of accuracy.

Extended

i. The range is $1.9 * 10^{-4951}$ to $11.1 * 10^{4932}$.

ii. It occupies ten bytes of memory and provides 19 or 20 digits of accuracy.

Comp

i. The range is from $-2^{63} +1$ to $2^{63} -1$.

ii. It occupies eight bytes of memory with accuracy equal to real type.

Char

It is defined as single character enclosed within single quote (')

'?'   'a' '#' are some of the valid char constants.

The declarations of char variable are as follows, provided i,j,k are assumed to be char variables.

VAR

i,j,k : Char;

Boolean

There are some circumstances where we want to have a logical value instead of an arithmetic one. The Boolean type makes it easier and allow us to store either true or false in it. It occupies one byte in memory. The declaration of Boolean type for making p,q,r as boolean variables is as follows.

VAR

p,q,r : Boolean;

PROCEDURES AND FUNCTIONS

Procedures and Functions have all the properties as the main program has but it can be executed only from the main program though it is a self contained program. Hence it is referred as a sub–program. The main advantage of using Structured programming is that we can split up a program into several individual modules (Procedures and Functions) and each one having a specific purpose. This will help us to scan and debug the program. So, any Procedure or Function which takes part in the program should also be defined before the main program starts. The Procedure and Function can be seen in detail in Chapter 6.

STATEMENTS

It is the place where all of our actions take place i.e. Read, Write and decision –making.

The structure that we have seen in the first page of this chapter clearly depicts how a typical Pascal program looks like.

Identifier

It is nothing but a program element which may be a

    Program name
    Function name
    Constant name
    Variable name.

and the rules for framing such a name will be the same as that of the program name. Some of the valid and invalid identifiers along with reasons are given below:

Valid Identifiers

    area, volume, tax_rate, incometax, string80

Invalid Identifiers

    1tree (First letter must be an alphabet)
    tax+rate (Special characters are not allowed)
    special price (here blank is not allowed between special and price)

Pascal also supports some standard (predefined) identifiers for specific purposes. The program may loose its charm if we redefine standard identifiers in our program and hence it is avoided. The list of standard identifiers are given below for reference.

PREDEFINED IDENTIFIERS

Addr	EOF	LightMagenta	Red
Append	EOLN	LightRed	Release
ArcTan	Erase	Ln	Rename
Assign	Execute	Io	Reset
Aux	Exit	Long File Pos	Rewrite
AuxInPtr	Exp	Long File Seek	Rmdir
AuxOutPtr	False	Long Seek	Round
Black	Filepos	Low Video	Seek
BlockRead	Filesize	Lst	Seg
BlockWrite	Fillchar	Lst OutPtr	SeekEof
Blue	Flush	Magenta	SeekEoln
Boolean	Frac	Mark	Sin
Brown	GetDir	MaxInt	Sizeof
Buflen	GetMem	Mem	Sqr
Byte	GotoXY	MemW	Sqrt
Chain	GraphBack ground	Memavail	Str
Char	GraphColorMode	Mkdir	SSet
Chdir	Graphmode	Move	Succ
Chr	GraphWindow	MsDos	Swap
Close	Green	New	Text
ClrEOL	Halt	NormVideo	Textbackground
Clrscr	HeapPtr	Odd	TextColor
Con	Hi	Ofs	Textmode
ConInPtr	Hires	Ord	Trm
ConOutPtr	HiResColor	Output	True
Concat	IOresult	Ovrpath	Trunc
ConstPtr	Input	Palette	UpCase
Copy	Insline	Pi	Usr
Cos	Insert	Plot	UsrInPtr
CrtExit	Int	Port	UsrOutPtr
CrtInit	Integer	PortW	Val
CSeg	Intr	Pos	WhereX
Cyan	Kbd	Pred	WhereY
Darkgray	KeyPressed	Ptr	White
Delline	Length	Random	Write
Delay	LightBlue	Randomize	Writeln
Delete	LightCyan	Read	Yellow
Draw	LightGray	Readln	
Dseg	LightGreen	Real	

RESERVED WORDS

The following is a list of reserved words in Turbo Pascal, and they should not be redefined by the programmer.

absolute	external	nil	shl
and	file	not	shr
array	forward	overlay	string
begin	for	of	then
case	function	or	type
const	goto	packed	to
div	inline	procedure	until
do	if	program	var
downto	in	record	while
else	label	repeat	with
end	mod	set	xor

EXPRESSION

It is a collection of variables, constants and operators. Consider the following arithmetic expression

$$x^2 + 5x + 6$$

The above expression consists of X as variable and 2, 5 and 6 as constants and these are connected by + operator.

Strings

It is a sequence of letters enclosed in a single quote. Number of letters in the string varies from implementation to implementation and most of the system will have an upper limit as 255, Some examples of string constants are given below.

'Cray XMP–14'

'Madurai–625 001'

A string without characters is considered to be a null string or empty string and such a string will be used to initialise the string variables. TURBO PASCAL also supports fixed length string and it assumes to be 255 if the length is not given in the declaration.

VAR

str : String ;

str1 : String [10];

In the above declaration str can hold a maximum of 255 characters and str1 will have only 10 characters in it. [Turbo Pascal Version 3.0 allows only fixed length string]

Operators

Pascal is equipped primarily with three types of operators. They are: arithmetic operator, relational operator and logical operator, and they are given in the following table.

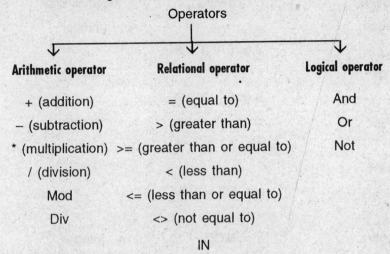

Arithmetic operator	Relational operator	Logical operator
+ (addition)	= (equal to)	And
– (subtraction)	> (greater than)	Or
* (multiplication)	>= (greater than or equal to)	Not
/ (division)	< (less than)	
Mod	<= (less than or equal to)	
Div	<> (not equal to)	
	IN	

In arithmetic operators, Mod and Div are the only two with which we are not much familiar. Now let us discuss about these two operators with suitable examples.

MOD :

It is used to get Remainder after division in integer operands

examples:

    5 MOD 3 leads to 2
    3 MOD 5 leads to 3

DIV

It is used to get quotient in integer operands.

Examples:

    5 DIV 3 leads to 1
    3 DIV 5 leads to 0

In relational operators the only operator which we are not aware is IN, it is used only in set comparison and it will be discussed in Chapter 9.

There are two types of arithmetic in Pascal since there are two data types existing for numbers. They are integer arithmetic and real arithmetic. Following table will clearly show a path of how it should be properly used to get a correct result.

Integer Arithmetic

Operands	Operator	Resultant type
Integer	+	Integer
	e.g. 5 + 3 = 8	
Integer	−	Integer
	e.g. 5 − 3 = 2	
Integer	*	Integer
	e.g. 5 * 3 = 15	
Integer	/	Real
	e.g. 5/3 = 1.66	
Integer	MOD	Integer
	e.g. 5 MOD 3 = 2	
Integer	DIV	Integer
	e.g. 5 DIV 3 = 1	

Real Arithmetic

Operands	Operator	Resultant type
Real	+	Real
	e.g. 5.0 + 3.0 = 8.0	
Real	−	Real
	e.g. 5.0 − 3.0 = 2.0	
Real	*	Real
	e.g. 5.0 * 3.0 = 15.0	
Real	/	Real
	e.g. 5.0/ 3.0 = 1.66	

Again the readers are reminded that the operators MOD and DIV should be used only in conjunction with integer operands and will yield compilation error if it is used with reals.

EXPONENT

In Turbo Pascal exponentiation is done in a different way. Usually BASIC and FORTRAN have an operator for it. Here exponentiation is carried out by using library functions (Built in functions). The functions involved in this process are Log and Exp. For example to find x^5 the following conversion should be used.

$$x^5 = \exp(5*\ln(X))$$

and for

$$x^{0.5} = \exp(0.5*\ln(X))$$

The function for finding the natural logarithm (base e) is Ln( ) in Turbo Pascal.

Assignment Statement

In declaration part we have seen how to declare integer, real, char and boolean variables. Initially all the variables just declared will have some arbitrary value in memory. So a variable should be defined with appropriate value before it takes part in any calculation. This can be accomplished by the assignment statement and it takes the following general form.

$$Var := expression ;$$

e.g.

```
amount := 8790 ;
area := 22.0/7.0 * radius * radius ;
Yesno := 'Y' ;
paid := true ;
```

Compilation error will occur when real value is assigned to integer variable and character is assigned to real. Also note that the symbol := is used to define a value to a variable and it should not be confused with the relational operator = which means equal to.

Data types

Pascal comes with three data types and they are as follows :

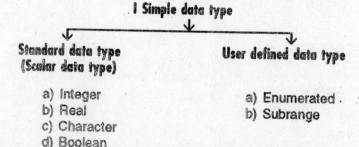

I Simple data type

Standard data type (Scalar data type)
- a) Integer
- b) Real
- c) Character
- d) Boolean

User defined data type
- a) Enumerated
- b) Subrange

The standard type data is also called fundamental data type.

II. Structured data type

  a) Arrays
  b) Records
  c) Files
  d) Sets

III. Pointer data type

In this chapter we have seen only Standard type data and remaining will be seen in the coming chapters in more detail.

Exercises

1.   Describe different data types used in PASCAL ? Give an example for each.

2.   What is an identifier ? Give the rules to define an identifier.

3.   What is the value of I calculated in the following assignment statement?

   J=3, K=6
   i) I:= J * 2 DIV 3 + K DIV 4 + 6 – J * J * J DIV 8
   ii) I := J DIV 2 * 4 + 3 DIV 8 + J * J * J

4.   Explain why the following identifiers are incorrect

   a) 1/4   b) 40,943.65   c) RS–PS   d) CONST
   e) 3 DOWN   f) LIGHT – SPEED   g) BEGIN   h) AREA.4
   i) Taxrate   j) ARRAY   H) LAST WORD

5.   What will be the value of the Pascal Expression:

   4 + 6 DIV 3 * 2 –2

6.   Identify errors, if any in the following

   a) **CONST**
      TEN   =   10 ;
      X   =   TEN :

   b) **CONST**
      A = 3 * 3 ;

   c) **LABEL**
      st,ak,25.5

   d) **VAR**
      X,Y,IF : Integer ;

7. Evaluate the following expressions

   a) 9 DIV 2 + 15 MOD 6
   b) 10 MOD 3 + 5 MOD 2

8. Summarize the complete structure of a PASCAL program.

9. It is expected to get the value of $8^{0.6}$ which of the following expressions is correct?

   a. 8 ** 0.6
   b. ln (0.6 *exp (8))
   c. exp (0.6*ln(8))

10. What is an expression ? When it is called

   i) an arithmetic expression
   ii) a boolean expression

11. What are the various basic declaration statements in Pascal?

12. Evaluate the expression with a=10, c=7, p='d'

   i) a+103 div sqr (a–c)

   ii) Chr (succ (ord(p)))

13. Explain the Pros and Cons of using structural data types in programming.

14. Can Literals and Constants be freely mixed with variables to form expressions?

CHAPTER - 3

INPUT–OUTPUT STATEMENTS

The purpose of writing a Computer program is to get correct result by entering relevant data for it. To feed data or to receive results from the Computer, the input and output statements are essential. Pascal is provided with some standard identifiers for this purpose and it will be discussed in the following sections.

READ, READLN are the two standard identifiers used to feed data to a program. The simplest form of these two standard identifiers are as follows.

```
READ (Var.list);
READLN (Var.list) ;
```
e.g.

```
READ (b,h);
READLN (p,n,r);
```

WRITE, WRITELN are other two standard identifiers used to receive results from the system. The general form for these two standard identifiers are as follows.

```
WRITE (Var. list) ;
WRITELN (Var. list);
```
e.g.

```
WRITE (i,j,k);
WRITELN (l,m,n);
```

At this moment, we will consider only READLN for input and WRITELN for output and later in this Chapter the difference between READ, READLN and WRITE, WRITELN will be dealt with.

READLN

Consider the following Readln statement.

```
Readln (a,b,c);
```

Assume that if a, b and c were integers and if they take 10, 20 and 30 respectively as values then we have to enter values for a, b and c in the following form.

```
10 20 30
```
Here a blank space is used to separate the values.

If a, b and c were real and have the values 10, 34.6 and 67.89 then the entering of values to corresponding variables is as follows.

    10 34.6 67.89

Please note that the first value (10) is entered as integer even though the variable a is real and decimal point is optional for reals if it has only integral part.

WRITELN

Consider the following Writeln statement.

```
Writeln(x,y,z);
```

If x, y and z were integers and the values for x, y and z were 123, 456 and 789, then it will display the result in the following manner.

```
123 456 -789
```

if x, y and z were reals with the same values the output will be in the following form.

```
1.2300000000E+02 4.5600000000E+02-7.8900000000E+02
```

Note that reals are always displayed in an exponential form, and formatted output if needed, the following general form is used for reals.

Var-name: total-width:no-of-decimals

if the value of P is 789.762 and it is asked to print the value in the following form

```
Writeln (p:8:2);
```

then the output will be

```
789.76
```

It is time for us to write a simple program by using the above rudiments. The simple rules to be followed while writing a program are as follows.

i.   First analyse the problem.

ii.   Convert the algebraic expression into Pascal expression if there is any expression involved in the program.

iii. Write a program and test it with different set of values.

The example program taken here is, to find the area of a triangle using the formula

area = 1/2bh

Here the input to the program is the base(b) and height(h) and the result is area.

First convert the formula into Pascal form

area = 0.5 * base * height

Since fractional part appears in the formula the result (area) should be in real form.

First stage of our program

```
Readln(base, height);
area:= 0.5 * base * height ;
Writeln(area);
```

The above statements are in simple form and we have to make it into compound form and it is done by using begin and end.

Second stage

```
begin
   Readln (base, height);
   area:= 0.5 * base * height ;
   Writeln (area);
end.
```

As we know already, every variable taking part in the program should be declared in the declaration part. Our program turns into the following form.

Third stage

```
Var
   area, base, height : real;
begin
     ReadIn(base,height);
     area:= 0.5 * base * height ;
     Writeln(area);
end.
```

Finally the program should be rewritten after including the header. The complete program takes the following form.

Final stage

```
Program findarea (input, output);
```

```
Var
   area, base, height : real;
begin
      Readln(base,height);
      area:= 0.5 * base * height ;
      Writeln(area);
end.
```

Output

    12 5

      3.0000000000E+01

The result obtained in the above program is in the exponential form. The formatted output can be obtained by changing the

      Writeln(area) ;

into

      Writeln (area:8:2);

The above output statement will print area in the format as 8:2, i.e. the total width of the area is 8 and number of decimal places after the decimal point is 2.

Output.

    12 5

      30.00

Comment entry

We can also have some meaningful heading to our program and such a comment entry (remarks) is given in two different ways.

   i) by enclosing comments in (* .... *)

   ii) by enclosing within { ..... }

Examples

   (* Program to find area of a triangle *)

   {Calculation of Income tax for the salaried people}

MORE ABOUT READ, READLN AND WRITE, WRITELN

Now we will discuss about the differences between Read, Readln and Write, Writeln.

READ, READLN

Let us consider the values arranged in the following fashion.

1 2 3 4 5 6	data line 1
10 11 8 9	data line 2
7 12 13	data line 3

and if the Read statements are

```
Read (a,b,c);
Read (d,e,f);
Read (i,j);
```

If the Read statement is executed it continues to assign the values to the subsequent Read also. Then the values to the above Read statements are given below.

a=1, b=2, c=3, d=4, e=5, f=6, i=10, and j=11

Now if all the three Read statements are changed into Readln as follows,

```
Readln(a,b,c);
Readln(d,e,f);
Readln(i,j);
```

Then after assigning a=1, b=2 and c=3 the remaining values in the first data line are skipped. Now d,e and f get 10,11 and 8 respectively. As readln is executed the remaining value in the second data line is also skipped. Finally i and j receive their values 7 and 12 from the third data line. From this one can understand that if readln is executed it will consider only that number of values as required by that readln statement.

What happens if both read and readln is executed as in the following segment

```
Read (a,b);
Readln (d,e);
Read(f,g);
Readln (i,j);
```

Now value allocation to the above variables is as follows.

The variables a and b are assigned to 1 and 2 from the first data line. As read statement is executed it continues to supply the values in the current data line to the subsequent readln statement. Thus d and e received 3 and 4 respectively. After executing this readln, the remaining values are skipped. The third read statement receives the value 10 and 11 for f and g from second data line. The same process repeats and i and j get their values from the current data line as 8 and 9.

Write, Writeln

Assume the following assignments to the variables,

a=1, b=2, c=3, d=8, e=9, f=10, i=23 and j=89

The effect after executing the following write statements are as follows.

```
Write(a:2,b:2);
Write (c:2,d:2);
Write (e:2,f:3);
```

Output

1 2 3 8 9 10

The values for a(=1) and b(=2) are printed in the first line, and the values for subsequent output statements will also be on the first line. Hence all the values of the variables will be printed in a single line as above. Normally integer values will be printed continuously without leaving any space. To get a formated output as in real type it is given as above.

Instead of Write statements above if it were Writeln, then the output will be

```
Writeln(a:2,b:2);
Writeln(c:2,d:2);
Writeln(e:2,f:2);
```

Output

1 2

3 8

9 10

Now the values for a(=1) and b(=2) will be on the first line and after execution the spaces in first line will be skipped. Then the values for c and d will be printed in second line and finally the values for e and f will be on the third line.

From above it is observed that if Writeln is executed the spaces after printing values for the Writeln will be skipped.

Now let us see the effect what if both Write and Writeln were mixed as given below.

```
Write (a:2,b:2);
Writeln(c:2,d:2);
Write(e:3,f:3);
Writeln(i:3,j:3);
```

In this case the values for a and b will be printed in the first line and only after printing the values for c and d in the same line the spaces in the first line will be skipped as Writeln is executed. The second line consists values for e, f, i and j. By using the above rules, the output will look like

1 2　3　8

9 10 23 89

If a blank line is required between the two output statements a blank writeln is used to perform the same.

```
Writeln(a:2,b:2);
Writeln;
Writeln(c:2,d: 2);
```

Then the output will be

1　2

3　8

Some meaningful message can also be added to the Writeln statement within single quotes to enhance the output format. If a = 23 and the output statement is

```
Writeln('The Value of a is',a);
```

Then the output will be

The Value of a is 23

Some additional forms of both Read, Readln and Write, Writeln are also available and they will be seen in greater detail in next Chapters.

Exercises

1. Write down the differences between READ, READLN and WRITE, WRITELN with suitable examples.

2. Write a program which prints.

   a) the area of a rectangle of sides a and b

   b) the volume of a sphere of radius r

3. With usual notations, the formula for compound interest is given by $A = P (1 + I/100)^N$ if it is known that P = Rs 6780, I = 14 and N = 8. Write a program to find A.

4. Write a note on Pascal output statements.

5. In the following program what can one say about the assignment statement a:=b?

Program Test;

```
Var
     b : Real;
     x : Integer;
begin
   b : = 9.6;
   x : = b;
end.
```

a. It causes a runtime error.   b)   it causes compile–time error.

c. the variable x gets value 9.   d)   the variable x gets value 10.

6. What will happen when a READLN statement is preceded by a READ statement? Give an example.

7. Write a program which reads the co–ordinates of the vertices of a triangle and outputs the area of the triangle.

8. Write a program to read the radius and the height of a cylinder and find the area and the volume of the cylinder. The formulae are given below ($\pi = 22/7$)

   area of the curved surface = 2 * π * r * h

   total outer area = 2 * π * r * (r + h)

   Volume = π * r * r * h

9. Write a Program segment to read values of variable a, b from card one and c, d from next card and output the values according to the format.

   Value of a = xxxxb   Value of b = xxxx

   Value of e = xxxxbb   Value of d = xxxx

10. How do you represent a compound statement in Pascal.

SOLVED PROGRAMS

1. Write a Program to reverse a given 5 digit Integer number.

```
Program Example (Input, Output);
Var
   N,A,B,C,D,E : integer;
Begin
   Writeln ('Enter No To Reverse');
   Readln(N);
   A:= N mod 10;
   B:= (N div 10) mod 10;
   C:= (N div 100) mod 10;
   D:= (N div 1000) mod 10;
   E:= N div 10000;
   Writeln ('Reversed No');
   Writeln (A,B,C,D,E);
End.
```

Output

Enter No To Reverse
12345
Reversed No
54321

2. A motorcycle covers a distance of 48 km per litre of petrol consumption. The cost of petrol is 20.30 per litre. Write a program in PASCAL to calculate the cost of petrol to travel a distance of 145 km.

```
Program Example (Input, Output);
var
   TotCost, CostPerLitre  : Real;
   TotKm, KmPerLitre      : Integer;
Begin
   CostPerLitre  : = 20.30;
   KmPerLitre    : = 48;
   TotKm         : = 145;
   TotCost := TotKm/KmPerLitre * CostperLitre:
   WriteLn ('Total Charge, TotCost:6:2);
```

CHAPTER – 4

CONTROL STATEMENTS

Pascal is considered to be the first successful structured programming language. The reason for calling it so is that, it supports a variety of 'if' and looping constructs.

The control statements are widely used to support decision making processes. They largely depend upon a conditional test that determines the decision.

Basically the program structure falls into the following three categories. They are

I. SEQUENTIAL STRUCTURE

In this structure, statements are executed in a sequential manner and there is no deviation in any part of the program. The programs we have discussed so far fall under this category.

II. SELECTIVE STRUCTURE

In this structure we can alter the flow of the program either conditionally or un–conditionally. The statements used for this purpose are called branching statements. If the program flow deviates after checking some condition then that flow is said to be a conditional flow and if the transfer takes place blindly without checking any condition then it is said to be an un–conditional flow.

III. REPETITIVE STRUCTURE

This structure is also called as looping structure. If we want to execute a group of statements many times the above said construct is used.

IF statement:

This is one of the most powerful conditional control statements. The if statement can be used in different modes, depending upon the nature of the conditional test. The different forms of 'if' statements are:

   i) Simple if

   ii) Block if

   iii) Nested if

We shall discuss different 'if' constructs in the coming sections.

Simple IF statement

The syntax of a simple IF statement is

**if (boolean expression) then
statement;**

Here, the boolean expression is one which returns its result by logical values i.e., either **true** or **false.** If the boolean expression returns **true** then the following statement is executed and for **false** the execution starts from the next statement.

(e.g.)

```
if (a > b)   then
     Writeln (' a is greater than b ');


If   (Sales <= 1000) then
   Commn :=  sales * 2/100;
```

Simple if–else statement

We can also include an optional clause "else" along with the simple if statement. The general form is

**if (boolean expression) then
        statement
else
        statement;**

(e.g.)

```
if (English>=40) then
     Writeln ('Pass in English')
else
     Writeln ('Fail in English');
```

Please note that there is no semicolon before **else** and **else** is considered as an identifier if there is a semicolon before it.

The logical operators not, and, or are used to connect one boolean expression with another boolean expression.

(e.g.)

```
if (units>100) and (units <=200)
    Charge := units * 0.70;
```

Write a program to find the largest of given three numbers.

```
Program Example (Input, Output);
    Var
        a,b,c : Integer;
    Begin
        Writeln ('Enter 3 Values');
        Readln (a,b,c);
        If (a > b) and (a > c) then
            Writeln (' A is largest');
        If (b > a) and (b > c)then
            Writeln ('B is largest');
        If (c > a) and (c > b) then
            Writeln ('C is largest');
    End.
```

Output

```
Enter 3 Values
4   5   2
  B is largest
Enter 3 Values
4   3   2
  A is largest
Enter 3 Values
3   4   5
  C is largest
```

Another example follows to calculate the sales commission using If statement.

Calculate the sales commission for the given criteria :

Sales amount in Rs.	Sales commission
less than or equal to 1000	No commission
above 1000 but less than or equal to 2000	3% of sales
above 2000 but less than or equal to 5000	5% of sales

above 5000   8% of sales

```
Program Example (Input, Output);
Var
      Sales, Commn: Real;
Begin
      Writeln ('Enter Sales Value');
      Readln(Sales);
      If (Sales <=1000) then
            Commn:=0;
      If (sales > 1000 ) and (Sales <=2000)then
            Commn:=Sales*3/100;
      If (Sales > 2000) and (Sales <=5000) then
            Commn:=Sales *5/100;
      If (Sales > 5000) then
            Commn:=Sales*8/100;
      Writeln ('Commission Value : ',Commn:8:2);
End.
```

Output

Enter Sales Value
500
Commission Value : 0.00
Enter Sales Value
1500
Commission Value : 45.00
Enter Sales Value
2500
Commission Value : 125.00
Enter Sales Value
5500
Commission Value : 440.00

Logical constants are also assigned to variables provided if they are declared as boolean.

Assume that a, b and c are boolean variables

a:=60 > 90;   will assign false to a

b:=(a) or (true);   will assign true to b

c:=(a) and (b);   will assign false to c

Consider the following output statement,

```
Writeln ( 100 > 10);
```

the result for the above is true.

Now let us consider another set of statements when a = 34 and b = 90

```
Writeln(a>b);
Writeln(a<b);
Writeln(a=b);
```

The output for the above statements is

false
true
false

The following example program illustrates the usage of logical constants in more detail.

```
Program Example (Input, Output);
Var
     Tam, Eng, Mat : Integer;
     a,b,c : Boolean;
Begin
     Writeln ('Enter Tam, Eng, Mat Marks');
     Readln (Tam, Eng, Mat);
     a:=Tam >=40;
     b:=Eng >=40;
     c:=Mat >=35;
     If (a) and (b) and (c) then
        Writeln ('Pass In Exam')
     Else
        Writeln ('Fail In Exam');
End.
```

Output

Enter Tam, Eng, Mat Marks
45 56 65
Pass In Exam

Enter Tam, Eng, Mat, Marks
20 25 30
Fail In Exam

Also note that True and False are standard identifiers and they may also be used as variables. The following program illustrates how it can be redefined in a program.

```
Program Example (Input, Output);
Var
      True : Boolean;
Begin
      True := False:
      If (True) then
         Writeln ('Failure')
      Else
      Writeln ('Success');
End.
```

Output

Success.

Here first True is declared as boolean variable and defined as false. When this value is substituted in 'If' construct, the boolean expression returns to false. So, THEN part of the 'If' construct will not be executed and ELSE part of the 'IF' construct will be executed to print the message 'Success'.

Block if Statement

Here a group of statements will be executed if the boolean expression evaluates to true. The group of statements must be enclosed between Begin and End.

The General form is

if (boolean expression) then
       begin
          —————————————

          statements;
          —————————————

   end;

(e.g.1)

```
if (salary >= 12000) then
     begin
         itax := salary * 9/100;
         ptax := salary * 8/100;
     end;
```

here, if salary is greater than or equal to 12000 then itax is computed as 9% of salary and ptax as 8% of salary.

(e.g.2)

```
if (mat >= 35) and (com >=35) and (eco >= 35) then
begin
      Writeln ('Pass in Exam');
      total :=mat + eco + com;
      average := total /3;
      Writeln ('Total Marks :' , total);
      Writeln ('Average is :' ,average:5:2);
end;
```

In the above 'block if' construct, if all the three subjects are greater than or equal to 35 then the sequences of statements within the begin and end are executed.

In both the examples, if boolean expression evaluates to false then the control will be transferred to statement next to end.

Block if–else statement

This one is identical to a simple if–else, except that a group of statements follow the boolean expression.

The general form is

if (boolean expression) then
    begin
        statements;
    end
else
    begin
        statements;
    end;

(e.g.)

```
if (pcode=10) then
    begin
       com1 := sales * 5/100;
       inc1 := sales * 3/100;
    end
  else
    begin
       com1 :=sales * 4/100;
       inc1 := sales * 2/100;
    end;
```

Here the boolean expression is tested. If it evaluates to true then the group of statements followed by **if** are executed. If it is false then the group of statements followed by **else** part are executed.

```
Program Example (Input, Output);
Var
      Tam,Eng,Mat,Tot : Integer;
      Ave             : Real;
Begin
      Writeln ('Enter Tam, Eng, Mat Marks');
      Readln (Tam,Eng,Mat);
      If (Tam >=40) and (Eng >=40) and (Mat>=35)then
   Begin
         Writeln ('Pass In Exam');
         Tot := Tam + Eng + Mat ;
         Ave := Tot / 3;
         Writeln ('Total :' , Tot);
         Writeln ('Average :' , Ave:5:2);
   End
   Else
         Writeln ('Fail In Exam ');
   End.
```

Output

Enter Tam, Eng, Mat Marks
50 60 70
Pass In Exam
Total : 180
Average: 60.00

Enter Tam, Eng, Mat Marks
20 25 30
Fail In Exam

Nested if statement

This is the most important aspect of the "if" statement, and it may lead to confusion if not properly used.

The general form of nested **if** is

if (boolean expression) then
    statement

else if (boolean expression) then
      statement
    else
      statement;

A careful understanding is required to know which "else" associates with which "if", and it can be achieved by indenting a program. That is why, it was said earlier that misused nested **if** may lead to chaos.

Here is a program to illustrate the same.

Problem.

Write a program to calculate the income tax for the individuals. The criteria is given below.

(1)   Where the total income does not exceed Rs. 28,000   Nil

(2)   Where the total income exceeds Rs. 28,000 but does not exceed Rs. 50,000   20% of the amount by which the total income exceeds Rs. 28,000

(3)   Where the total income exceeds Rs. 50,000 but does not exceed Rs. 1,00,000   Rs. 4,400 plus 30% of the amount by which the total income exceeds Rs 50,000

(4)   Where the total income exceeds Rs. 1,00,000   Rs. 19,400 plus 30% of the amount by which the total income exceeds Rs. 1,00,000

```
Program Example (Input, Output);
Var
     Income, Tax : Real ;
Begin
     Writeln ('Enter Income');
     Readln(Income);
     If (Income <= 28000.00) then
        Tax := 0
     Else If (Income <=50000.00) then
        Tax := (Income - 28000.00) * 20/100
     Else If (Income <=100000.00) then
        Tax := (Income - 50000.00) * 30/100 + 4400
     Else
        Tax := (Income - 100000.00) * 40
```

```
                    Writeln ('Tax Amount ' ,Tax :8:2);
            End.
```

Output

Enter Income
20000
Tax Amount   **0.00**

Enter Income
30000
Tax Amount   **400.00**

Enter Income
75000.00
Tax Amount   **11900.00**

Enter income
125000.00
Tax Amount   **29400.00**

Block nested if

This is similar to the previous form, except that a block of statements follow the boolean expression.

The general form is

if (boolean expression) then
   begin
      statements;
   end
else if (boolean expression) then
   begin
      statements;
   end
else
      begin
         statements;
      end;

Example program to illustrate the block nested if follows.

```
Program Example (Input, Output);
Var
        Examno, Code, S1,S2,S3,S4,S5, Tot : Integer;
```

```
Begin
          Writeln ('Examno');
    Readln (Examno);
    Writeln('Enter Code 1 For 3 Subjects, 2 For 4 Subjects, 3 For 5 Subjects');
    Readln (Code);
    If (Code=1) Then
          Begin
                  Writeln ('Enter 3 Subjects Marks ');
                  Readln (S1,S2,S3);
                  Tot:=S1+S2+S3;

          End
    Else If (Code=2) Then
          Begin
                . Writeln('Enter 4 Subjects Marks');
                  Readln(S1,S2,S3,S4);
                  Tot :=S1+S2+S3+S4;

          End
    Else
          Begin
                  Writeln ('Enter 5 Subjects Marks');
                  Readln (S1,S2,S3,S4,S5);
                  Tot:=S1+S2+S3+S4+S5;

          End;
            Writeln ('Examno : ',Examno);
            Writeln ('Total : ',Tot);
End.
```

Output

Examno
101
Enter Code 1 For 3 Subjects, 2 For 4 Subjects, 3 For 5 subjects
1
Enter 3 Subjects Marks
50 60 70
Examno:101
Total :180

Examno
201
Enter Code 1 For 2 Subjects, 2 For 4 Subjects, 3 For 5 Subjects
2
Enter 4 Subjects marks
50 60 70 80
Examno: 201

Total : 260

Examno
301
Enter Code 1 For 3 Subjects, 2 For 4 Subjects, 3 For 5 Subjects
3
Enter 5 Subjects Marks
50 60 70 80 90
Examno:301
Total:350

Note that how coding has been reduced when the program is written using nested **if**. In this nested **IF**, if any of the boolean expression is evaluated to be true then the statement following it will be executed and control will be transferred to the last line of the if statement.

Looping Structure

Now let us turn our attention towards the looping constructs available in Pascal and how it helps to facilitate the program constructs.

In Pascal there are three types of looping structures available and we will scan it one by one with suitable illustrations.

i. WHILE–DO loop

This type of loop is also called an entry controlled loop statement, i.e., the boolean expression is evaluated and if it is true then the body of the loop is executed. This process is repeated until the boolean expression becomes false. Once it becomes false, the control is transferred out of the loop.

The general form of while–do loop is   In Flow chart form

While (boolean expression) do

begin

    statements;

end;

False

B.E. / False / True / BODY OF THE LOOP / NEXT STATEMENT

Now let us see what we have discussed, through an example:

Program to sum the series comprising of odd number.

1+3+5+7...100

```
Program Example (Input, Output);
Var
          I,Sum:Integer;
Begin
             I:=1;
             Sum:=0;
          While (I <=100)do
          Begin
             Sum:=Sum+I;
             I:=I+2;
          End;
      Writeln ('The Sum of odd Numbers Between 1-100 ',Sum);
End.
```

Output

The Sum of Odd Numbers Between 1–100 = 2500

Here the **sum** and **I** are initialised, before it enters into the loop, first boolean expression is tested, if it returns true then the statements within begin and end will be executed. Note that I gets incremented by 2 inside the loop, if it is missing then the loop is an infinite one as I is always less than 100.

Now consider the following While–do loop structure in which the loop is executed infinitely

```
a:=true;
While (a) do

  Begin

        Statements;

  End;
```

The following program demonstrates how an infinite loop is used in Pascal.

```
Program Example (Input, Output);
Var
```

```
              A:Boolean;
Begin
              A:= True;
              While (A) do
                        writeln ('Welcome To Turbo Pascal');
End.
```

Output

Welcome to Turbo Pascal
Welcome to Turbo Pascal
Welcome to Turbo Pascal
Welcome to Turbo Pascal

....

Here we have to use unconditional statement (GO TO) to make exit from such a loop.

ii REPEAT – UNTIL Loop

In REPEAT–UNTIL loop, the boolean expression is evaluated only after performing the body of the loop. If the condition is false then it executes the body of the loop again and again until the loop expression becomes true.

The simplest form of this loop is   In Flow chart from

Repeat

    Statements;

Until (Boolean expression);

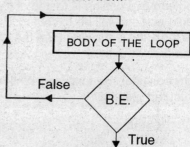

The following program is to find the sum of the series given below

1.0 + 1.1 + 1.2 + 1.3 + ...+ 2.5

```
Program Example(Input,Output);
Var
              N,Sum:Real;
Begin
              N:=1;
              Sum:=0;
```

```
        Repeat
                Sum:=Sum + N;
                N := N + 0.1;
        Until (N>=2.5);
Writeln ('The Series Sum is: ',Sum:6:2);
End.
```

Output

The Series Sum is: 28.00

Here the statements between Repeat–Until are executed first, and then the boolean expression is tested. So, there is a possibility of executing the statments between Repeat–Until at least once, even if the boolean expression does not satisfy the condition and this is the very basic difference between while–do and repeat–until loop.

Please note that there is no Begin and End between Repeat–Until loop because Repeat–Until itself acts as a bracket and hence no more Begin and End are needed.

Here is another program to illustrate the above construct in more detail.

Program to find the sum of the digits of a given number

```
Program Example (input,Output);
Var
        No,A,Sum :Integer;
Begin
        Writeln ('Enter Your Number ');
        Readln (No);
        Sum:=0;
        Repeat
            A:=No Mod 10;
            Sum :=Sum + A;
            No :=No Div 10 ;
        Until (No <1);
    Writeln ('The sum of the digits of a given number ',Sum);
End.
```

Output

Enter Your Number
156
The sum of the digits of a given number is :12

iii FOR loop

The For loop is used to repeat a single statement or group of statements for a specific number of times. Pascal has 2 types of **For loop** and we will discuss one by one.

a. FOR With TO Option

The general form of this type of loop is

For Index :=Initial–Value to Final–Value do

Statement;

Where

Index can be an integer or character or boolean variable and it cannot be a real variable. Index is also called as a running variable.

Initial–Value is the initial value for the index variable.

Final–Value is the final value for the index variable

For example to sum the numbers between 1 and 100 the following program construct may be used.

```
Sum:=0;
for i:= 1 to 100 do
     Sum := Sum + i;
```

The following steps involved in the above program are:

1. Initialisation
   (i.e. Assign initial–value to index)

2. Condition checking
   (If the initial–value is less than the final–value)

3. Execute the statement following do if the condition checking returns true.

4. Increment the index by 1

5. Repeat the process from step 2. If the condition checking returns false then come out of the loop

More than one statement may also be added by adding Begin and End after do and the general form is as follows.

For Index :=initial–value to final–value do
   Begin
      statements;
   End;

Example program to check whether the given number is Prime or Not.

```
Program Example (Input,Output);
Var
      No,A,I :Integer;
Begin
      Writeln('Enter No To Check');
      Readln(No);
      For I:=2 to No-1 do
            Begin
              A:=No Mod I ;
              If (A =0) then
                Begin
                  Writeln ('Given No is not a prime No ');
                  Exit;
                End;
            End;
      Writeln ('Given No is Prime No ');
End.
```
Output

Enter No To Check
7
Given No is Prime No

Enter No To Check
9
Given No is Not a Prime No

Once it is found that the given number is not a prime number after printing an appropriate message, the program should come to an end.

GO TO may be used to perform the above task. To avoid GO TO here EXIT (Predefined Identifier) is used to do the same job.

b. FOR With DOWNTO–DO Option

As we have said already, 'For' loops come in two forms and we have seen so far the first type. Here is the second type which is used to decrement the index by one.

The general form of "for–downto–do" is

For index :=Final–Value downto Initial–Value do
      Statement;

Let us see "for–downto–do" through an example

Program to find out the factorial of a given number.

```
Program Example (Input,Output);
Var
        Fact,No,I: integer;
Begin
        Writeln ('Enter Number to find factorial ');
        Readln(No);
        Fact:=1;
                For I:=No downto 1 do
                    Fact:=Fact * I;
    Writeln ('The Factorial of a Given Number is ',fact);
End.
```

Output

Enter Number to find factorial
5
The Factorial of a Given Number is 120

Here also, more than one statement can be added by adding **begin** and **end** after **do** and the general form is as follows.

For Index :=Final–value downto Initial–value do

  Begin

    Statements;

  End;

Rules to be observed in For loops

1.   The value of an index should not be changed within the body of the for loop, i.e., it cannot be either incremented or decremented. We will see what happens if we overrule this rule through an example program.

```
Program Example (Input, Output);
Var
        I:Integer;
Begin
        For I:= 1 to 10 do
            Begin
                I:=I+1;
                Writeln ('Welcome To Pascal Ver 5.5 ');
            End;
End.
```

Output

Welcome To Pascal Ver 5.5
Welcome To Pascal Ver 5.5
Welcome To Pascal Ver 5.5
Welcome To Pascal Ver 5.5
Welcome To Pascal Ver 5.5

Here the message 'Welcome To Pascal Ver 5.5' will be printed 5 times instead of 10 as the loop counter is altered within the body of the loop. Hence it is avoided.

2. In BASIC language, the loop will come out only if the index variable is greater than the final value, but it is not the case in PASCAL's 'for' loop. The value of index variable is the same even after the completion of the loop. This will be demonstrated by the following program.

```
Program Example (Input,Output);
Var
        I:Integer;
Begin
        For I:=1 to 5 do
            Writeln ('Welcome');
        Writeln (i);
End.
```

Output

Welcome
Welcome
Welcome
Welcome
Welcome

The value of I in the above is only 5 and it is not 6 as expected by you.

3.   There should be atleast one executable statement associated with the loop. If there is no action statements then the loop is said to be a "Time Delay Loop" or "Software Delay". This Kind of loop will be occasionally used to pause the program for a specific time.

```
For I:=1 to 1000 do;
```

Comparative study of the loop

It is upto the programmer's choice to choose the type of the loop. But before choosing the particular type, the following points should be considered. If the increment or decrement is either real or integer then we can use While–do or Repeat until loop. And also we want to execute the loop atleast once even though the condition is false then definitely we have to use Repeat–until loop. The for loop should be used only when the increment or decrement is 1 and it is very useful in Arrays.

CASE statement

This is a multiple branching control statement, and this type is very useful for decision making when more than one case is involved.

The general form of the CASE statement is

CASE expression of

Label 1:
    Begin
      statements;
    End;

Label 2:
    Begin
      statements;
    End;

Label 3:
    Begin
      statements;
    End;

Label n:
    Begin
      statements;
    End;

else
      Begin
        statements;
      End;
End;

The expression is either integer type or char type. When the Case statement is executed, the value of expression is compared with the label 1, label 2 etc., upto label n. If the value of expression matches with the label, then the sequence of statements that follow the label are executed. The **Else** statement is executed if no matches are found and it is optional.

Example program to illustrate the Case Statement.

```
Program Example (Input, Output);
Var
          Cho :Char;
          V1,V2:Integer;
Begin
          Writeln ('Enter Your Choice + , -, *, / ');
          Readln (Cho);
          Writeln ('Enter Two Values ');
          Readln (V1,V2);
            Case Cho of
            '+' : Writeln ('The result is ', V1 + V2);
            '-' : Writeln ('The result is ', V1 - V2);
            '*' : Writeln ('The result is ', V1 * V2);
            '/' : Writeln ('The result is ', V1 / V2 :7:2)
          Else
            Writeln ('Invalid choice. Try again ');
          End;
          Readln;
End.
```

Output

Enter Your Choice + , - , * , /
+
Enter Two Values
5 2
The result is 7

Enter Your Choice + , - , * , /
—

Enter Two Values
5 2
The result is 3

Enter Your Choice + , – , * , /
*

Enter Two Values
5 2
The result is 10

Enter Your Choice + , – , * , /
/
Enter Two Values
5 2
The result is 2.50

First we have to enter our choice of operators (+,–,*,/), and it is received by a character variable **cho.** Now we have to supply two operands to process. If entered choice does not belong to any one of the above four, the **ELSE** part of the Case statement is executed to display the message "Invalid Choice, Try again".

Please note that Cho in the case statement should not be of real type.

The following program segment is invalid one.

```
Case opt of
    1.0 : ...   ;
    2.0 : ...   ;
    3.0 : ...   ;
end;
```

Now consider the following code

```
Case x of
    1  : y:=y*7;
    3,5 :Y:=Y-2;
    2,3,4 : Y:=Y+10;
end;
```

In the above segment when x=1, y is multiplied by 7 and it is stored in y. When x=3 or x=5, y is subtracted by 2 and it is stored in y itself. If x=2 or x=3 or x=4, y is incremented by 10 and stored in y. From this example it is seen that the labels may also be combined to execute the same set of statements.

Another program which uses block construct in the CASE statement.

```
Program Example (Input,Output);
Var
        Centi, Fahren : Real;
        Opt           : Integer;
Begin
    Writeln ('Enter 1 for Centigrade to Fahrenheit ');
    Writeln ('       2 for Fahrenheit to Centigrade ' );
    Readln (Opt);
    Case Opt of

      1: Begin
         Writeln ('Enter Centigrade ');
         Readln (Centi) ;
         Fahren := 9/5 * centi + 32;
         Writeln ('Fahrenheit Temperature is:,Fahren:6:2);
         End;

      2: Begin
         Writeln ('Enter Fahrenheit ');
         Readln (Fahren);
         Centi := 5/9 * (Fahren - 32);
         Writeln ('Centigrade Temperature is : ' , Centi:6:2);
         End;

    End;

End.
```

Output

Enter 1 for Centigrade to Fahrenheit
     2. for Fahrenheit to Centigrade
1
Enter Centigrade
40
Fahrenheit Temperature is: 104.00

Enter 1 for Centigrade to Fahrenheit
     2 for Fahrenheit to Centigrade

2
Enter Fahrenheit
104
Centigrade Temperature is: 40.00

Goto statement

This is the only unconditional statement available in Turbo Pascal. Our main aim in the structured programming is to avoid unusual **goto** which may lead to confusion. But, the **goto** statement may be used to exit from several layers of nesting. The general form of **Goto** statement is

   Goto label;

where label may be numeric or alphanumeric, and it is declared before the const declaration, e.g.

```
Program example ;
label 100;
Const
        X = 25;
begin

        _____

        _____

        goto   100;
        _____

100:
        _____

end.
```

The use of 'goto' is not encouraged since more number of 'goto' means more confusion.

Exercises

1. Narrate the structure and functions of IF statement.

2. Write a program to list first 100 prime numbers.

3. Write a program in Pascal to find roots of a quadratic equation using CASE statement.

4. Write the equivalent of

FOR J := 1 TO N DO

BEGIN

<STATEMENTS>

END;

Using while–do construct.

5. Explain the REPEAT–UNTIL structure. How does it differ from the WHILE–DO structure? Explain with suitable examples.

```
6. Program test;
        var
           j:integer;
        begin
           j:=1;
           while (j < 50) do
              begin
                 writeln ('Welcome');
                      j:=j*j+1;
              end;
        end.
```
How many times will 'Welcome' be printed ?

```
7. Program test;
      var
         i,j,k,i, c:integer;
      begin
         i:=1;
         c:=0;
         j:=1;
         k:=10;
         c:=100;
```

```
      for I:= 1 to k*k do
      begin
           k:=k+20;
           c:=c+1;
      end;
           writeln (c);
   end.
```

What will be the output when the program is executed?

8. To be included in a cricket team the age should not be less than 20 and should not be greater than 25.

   The program segment to accomplish this is

   a) if (age >=20) or (age<=25)then
          writeln('included');

   b) if (((age −20)*(age −25)) < 0) then
          writeln('included ');

   c) if (((age −20)*(age −25)) < 0) then
          writeln('included ');

   d) if (((age −20)*(age −25)) < 0) then
          writeln('included ');

9.
```
   Program test;
   var
      m,n:integer;
   begin
      m:=o;
      n:=o;
      while(n <= 60) do
        begin
              m:=m+2;
              if ( m > 20)then
              begin
                 writeln(n);
                 exit;
              end;
        end;
      writeln(n);
   end.
```

What will be the output when the program is executed?

```
10.   Program test;
      var
            m,n:integer;
      begin
            m:=5;
            for n:=1 to m do
            begin
              m:=4;
              writeln('m');
            end;
      end.
```
What will be the output when the program is executed?

```
11.   Program test;
      var
            i,j,k,m,:integer;
      begin
            m:=0;
            j:=10;
            k:=1;
            for i:= 1 to j do
            begin
              k:= -2;
              m:=m+i;
              i:=i+k;
            end;
      writeln(m);
      end.
```
What will be the output when the program is executed?

```
12.   Program test;
      var
            s,m:integer;
      begin
            s :=5;
            for m:= 100 downto 0
      .     begin
              s:=s+3;
              s:=s-2;
            end;
      writeln(m);
      end.
```
What will be the output when the program is executed?

13.
```
program test;
var
        a,b,c,d:real;
begin
        a:=6.9;
        b:=2.4;
        c:=10;
        d:=5;
        if (a > 6.9) then c:=c+d;
        if (c <= 25) then d:=d-c;
        if (c =10 ) then b:=a+c;
        if (d <=0) then b:=d+a;
        Writeln (c:5:2,d:5:2);
end.
```
What will be the output when the program is executed?

14. Consider the following program block.

```
a:=2;
b:=1.5+a;
c:=a/(b+0.5);
for i:= 1 to 3 do
   begin
      a:=a+c;
      writeln(c:10:3,a:10:3);
   end;
```
What will be the output when the program is executed?

15. Consider the following program block.

```
for i:= 1 to 5 do
for j:= 1 to i do
for k:= 1 to j do
   begin
      writeln ('welcome');
   end;
```
When a program using this segment is executed, how many times will the message 'welcome' be executed?

16. Consider the following program

```
Program test;
var
   j: Integer;
Begin
```

```
        for j:= 1 to 10 do
            begin
                j:= j+1;
                writeln ('welcome to pascal ');
            end;
    End.
```

How many times will the string 'welcome to pascal ' be printed?

17. Consider the following program

```
        If c < 0
            then
                begin
                    if d < 0
                        then
                            d:=d+1
                        else
                            c:=a+1;
                end;
```

What is the value of c after the above segment is executed, if initially c = 9 and d = 89.

18. Write a PASCAL program which calculates

   1/1 + 1/3 + 1/5 + 1/7 ..... 1/21

19. Write a program in Pascal to find the sum of the N terms of the series.

   $S = 1 + X + X^2 + X^3 + ... X^N$ for the given value of X.

20. Write a program to print the multiplication table of order N.

21. Write a Pascal program to print the factorial value of numbers from 5 to 15.

22. Write a Pascal program to print the sum of the first 20 multiples of 12.

23. Suppose that H, M and N are variables of the type integer, identify the job of the following compound statement is designed to do.

```
        BEGIN
            WHILE (M <> 0) AND (N <> 0 ) DO
                IF (M < N) THEN N:= N MOD M
                        ELSE M:= M MOD N
                IF (M = 0) THEN H:= N ELSE H:= M
```

Explain your answer by choosing suitable specific values for M and N.

24. Write a Pascal program to evaluate the series

$$s = 1 - \frac{x^2}{2^2 . 1.1} + \frac{x^4}{2.^4 . 2!.2!} - \frac{x^6}{2^6 . 3!.3!}$$

25. Specify the syntax of the case statement. Also specify the important rules associated with the statement. Explain its logic.

26. Consider the following program segment.

```
i := 6728 ;
j := 5 ;
While (( i mod j) = 0) Do
Begin
    i := i div j;
    j := j + 1 ;
End;
```

What is the value of j after the above segment is executed?

27. In the following Pascal program segment, what is the value of X after the execution of the program segment.

X := −10 ; Y :=20;

if X > Y THEN IF X < 0 then X := abs (X) else X := 2 * X

a)   10   b) −20   c) −10   d) None of the above.

28. Assume that X and Y are nonzero positive integers. What does the following Pascal program segment do?

```
While X <> Y do
if X > Y then
    X : X - Y
else
    Y := Y - X;
write (X);
```

a)   Compute the LCM of two numbers

b)   Divide the larger number by the smaller number

c)   Compute the GCD of two numbers

d)   None of the above.

SOLVED PROBLEMS

1. Write a Pascal program to find the roots of a quadratic equation. Include all possibilities.

```
Program Example (Input,Output);
Var
    A,B,C,Disc, Root1,Root2: Real;
Begin
    Writeln ('Enter A,B,C ');
    Readln(A,B,C);
    Disc := B*B -4*A*C;
    If (Disc < 0) then
     Begin
      Writeln ('Real and Positive Roots ');
      Root1 := (-B + Sqrt (Disc)) / ( 2 * A );
      Root2 := (-B - Sqrt (Disc)) / ( 2 * A );
      Writeln ('Root1 = ',Root1:8:2, Root1:8:2, Root2=',Root2:8:2);
     End
     Else If (Disc = 0) then
       Begin
         Writeln ('Equal Roots ');
         Root1 :=  -B / ( 2 * A );
         Root2 := Root1 ;
         Writeln ('Root1 = ' ,Root1:8:2,  Root2= ', Root2:8:2);
       End
     Else
       Begin
         Writeln ('Complex  Roots ');
         Disc := - Disc;
         Root1 :=   Sqrt (Disc) / ( 2.0 * A );
         Root2 :=   -B / (2.0 * A);
         Writeln ('Root1 = ' ,Root1:8:2,  Root2= ', Root2:8:2);
       End;
End.
```

Output

Enter A, B, C
3 4 5
Complex roots
Root1 = 1.11 Root2 = –0.67

Enter A, B, C
2 6 3
Real and Positive Roots
Root1 = –0.63 Root2 = –2.37

Enter A, B, C
2 4 2
Equal Roots
Root1 = –1.00 Root2 = –1.00

2. Write a Pascal Program that sum up the following series.

   –1, +2, –4, +8, –16, ... +1024.

```
Program Example (Input , Output);
Var
        N, Sum, Sign, Prod : Integer;
Begin
        Prod : 1 ;
        Sum : 0 ;
        Sign := -1 ;
        While (Prod <= 1024) do
          Begin
                Sum := Sum + Sign * Prod ;
                Sign := -Sign ;
                Prod := Prod *2 ;
          End;
Writeln ('The sum of The Series', Sum );
End.
```

Output

The Sum of The Series – 683

3. Write Pascal statements for computing the value of a real variable
   'm' to the power of a positive integer 'n'.

```
Program Example (Input, Output);
Var
        M,Sum : Real;
        N,I : Integer;
Begin
        Writeln ('Enter Value ');
        Readln (m);
        Writeln ('Enter Power ');
        Readln (N);
```

```
        Sum :=1;
        I :=1;
        While (I <=N ) do
           begin
                  sum := Sum * M ;
                  I := I = 1;
             end;
   Writeln ('M To The power of a positive integer N Is,'Sum:8:2);
End.
```

Output

Enter Value
4
Enter power
2
M To The power of a positive integer N Is 16.00

4. Develop an interactive program in Pascal which prompts the user for a 3 digit integer and checks whether the middle digit is numerically equal to the sum of the other two digits and prints an appropriate response.

```
Program Example   (Input,Output);
Var
    No, A,B,C :  Integer;
Begin
    Writeln ('Enter No');
    Readln(No);
    A:=No Mod 10;
    B:=(No Div 10) Mod 0;
    C:=No Div 100;
    If (B = (A+C) then
     Writeln('Extreme Numbers Are Numerically Equal To Middle No')
    Else
     Writeln ('Extreme Numbers Are Not Numerically Equal To Middle No');
End.
```

Output

Enter No
132
Extreme Numbers Are Numerically Equal To Middle No

Enter No
456
Extreme Numbers Are Numerically Equal To Middle No

5.   Write a Program to calculate the sum of the series
      1/2 + 3/4 + 5/6 + − ....+ 99/100

```
Program Example (Input, Output);
Var
          I,J : Integer;
          Sum : Real;
Begin
          Sum := 0;
          I := 1  ; J := 2;
          While (I <= 99) And ( J <= 100) Do
            Begin
                  Sum := Sum + I/J;
                  I := I+2;
                  J := J+2;
            End;
          Writeln ('The Sum is ', Sum :8:4);
End.
```

Output

The Sum is 47.7504

6.   Write a program to test the divisibility by both 3 and 7 of a number
      (between 1–100)

```
Program Example (Input, Output);
Var
          I,J,K : Integer;
Begin
          For I := 1 to 100 Do
            Begin
                  J := I Mod 3;
                  K := I Mod 7;
              If (J=0) And (K=0) Then
                  Writeln (I);
            End;
End.
```

Output

21
42
63
84

7.   Write a program to find X^r for a given X.

```
Program Example (Input, Output);
Var
        X,R,Sum : Real;
Begin
        Writeln ('Enter Value for X ');
        Readln (X);
        R := 1;
        Sum := 0;
        While (R <= 10) Do
           Begin
                Sum := Sum + Exp (R * Ln (X));
                R:= R+!;
           End;
           Writeln ('The Sum is ', Sum : 7:2);
End.
```

Output

Enter Value for X
2
The sum is 2046.00

CHAPTER - 5

ARRAYS

So far, we have oriented ourselves to Simple Data Types and have learned about control statements. Now, we can move to the next data type called "Structured".

Structured data type consists of Arrays, Records, Files and Sets. In this chapter we will discuss the advantages of using Arrays.

Usually, all simple data type variable can store only one value at a time and if we want to store a new value in the same variable then we have to erase the previous one. But there are occasions where we want to store more than one value to a particular variable. This could be accomplished by using Arrays.

An array is a collection of variables of the same data type and it is referenced by a common name. Let us consider a real time situation where it is fully utilised. In our class there are 20 students and every body takes physics examination. Now we want to assign 20 values for the variable physics. Here the marks obtained by the students are different but all of them are referred by the same variable 'Physics'. In this situation we are in need of Arrays and the general form of an Array is

Var

ARRAY–NAME: ARRAY [LOWER–BOUND .. UPPER–BOUND] of DATA TYPE;

So, our declaration for the above case takes the form as

Var

PHYSICS : ARRAY [1..20] of INTEGER;

On executing the above declaration, the system will reserve 20 memory location for the identifier Physics and it is represented as follows:

Physics [1]   Physics [2]   Physics[20]

Here the index starts from 1 and goes upto 20.

The above type of ARRAY is called a one–dimensional array, and it is also called a "List". This means that an element in an array can be accessed by just giving an index or subscript. Arrays may have one to several dimensions and we will discuss each in detail later.

Several examples showing the one-dimensional array declaration are given below;

Var

AVERAGE : ARRAY [1...10] of REAL;

Declares the average as an array containing 10 real elements.

Var

RESULT : ARRAY [1..10] of CHAR ;

Declares the Result as a character array containing 10 character elements.

Var

NAME : ARRAY [1..10] of STRING [20];

Declares location for 10 names and each one will have 20 characters in it.

Let us see through an example program.

Problem:

To find the maximum number and its position in an array.

```
Program Example (Input,Output);
Var
        N               : Array [1..10]of Integer;
        I,Max, Maxpos : Integer
Begin
        Writeln ('Enter 10 numbers 1 by 1 ');
        For i:=1 to 10 do
          Readln (N[I]);
            Max:=N[1];
            Maxpos :=1 ;
        For i:=2 to 10 do
        if (max < N[i]) then
            begin
            Max :=N[i];
```

```
                    Maxpos := i;
                    end;
    Writeln ('The Maximum Number is ', Max, ' Its position is ', maxpos);
End.
```

Output

Enter 10 numbers 1 by 1
345
76
12
786
87
112
324
562
478
512
The Maximum Number is 786 Its position is 4

Explanation

The algorithmic approach is given below :

Step 1 : read the 10 elements one by one.

step 2 : Initialise

$$Max = N[1]$$

$$Maxpos = 1$$

Step 3 : Repeat Step 4 Varying I from 2 to 10

Step 4 : If max , N (I) then

$$Max = N [I]$$

$$Maxpos = I$$

Step 5 : Print max, maxpos

Here is yet another example to illustrate the usage of arrays in everyday affairs. If we want to arrange 10 names or numbers in a required manner i.e. either in ascending sequence or in descending sequence we can make use of the capabilities of arrays. For doing such a process we need a sorting algorithm, and sorting is a method of arranging a list of quantities (of the same data type) in a desired manner.

At present many algorithms are available for doing the above job. The most popular and important algorithms are given below :

1. Quick Sort
2. Bubble Sort
3. Shell Sort
4. Insertion Sort
5. Selection Sort

Here we are considering the Bubble sort method for illustration.

Assume that we are provided with two numbers say, 17 and 33. For this no sorting process is required as it is trivial to arrange them either in ascending or descending order. Now consider the case where there are three numbers, to be arranged in an ascending order

14 89 12

Here, first we are comparing the first number with the second one i.e. 14 with 89 and find that they are in ascending order. Now we compare the first number with the third number i.e. 14 with 12. They are not in ascending sequence and in this case we interchange their position as follows :

12 89 14

We have got the lowest number in the first position after performing two comparisons. Our job will be over if we place the next lowest number in the second position. Now we compare the second number with the third number i.e., 89 with 14. Here also the numbers are not in ascending sequence and we therefore interchange the positions as before. Thus the final display will be as follows :

12 14 89

The same approach will be followed even if we sort N numbers. It is to our benefit that we understand how interchanging takes place. The process of changing the values between two variables is called swapping.

For example, if
a = 12 and b = 89

and if we want our output as

a = 89 and b = 12

We use a third variable 't' as a temporary one. Then the following will be the sequence of coding to exchange the values between the two variables.

$$t := a ;$$

$$a := b ;$$

$$b := t ;$$

The first line of coding will assign the value of **a**(=12) to the temporary variable **t**. The second line of coding will assign the value of **b**(=89) to 'a' after erasing the previous value of **a** i.e., 12. The last line of coding will assign the temporary value (=12) to **b** after erasing the previous value of **b** i.e. 89. And the output will be

a = 89 and b = 12

Now let us code a Pascal program to arrange 5 numbers by implementing the Bubble sort method.

```
Program Example (Input,Output);
Var
                N: Array [1..5] of Integer;
           I,J,K,Temp : Integer;
Begin
           Writeln('Enter 5 numbers ');
           For i:= 1 to 5 do
              Readln(N[i]);
           For i:= 1 to 4 do
              For j:= i+1 to 5 do
                 if (N[i] > N[j]) then
                    begin
                        Temp := N[i];
                        N[i] := N[j];
                        N[j] := Temp;
                    end;
Writeln('The Sorted Nos are ');
           For i:= 1 to 5 do
                Writeln (N[i]);
End.
```

Output

Enter 5 numbers
874
234

112
87
93

The Sorted Nos are
87
93
112
234
874

Let us now discuss about the four fundamental operations on linear Arrays (One dimensional arrays)

I. Traversing an array

It is nothing but scanning or viewing an entire array contents.

The following program will show how array elements can be viewed.

```
Program Example (Input, Output);
Var
          N ; Array [1..5] of integer;
          i : integer;
Begin
          Writeln('Enter 5 Numbers');
          For i = 1 to 5 do
            Readln(N[i]);
          Writeln('The Entered Numbers are');
          For i:=1 to 5 do
            Write (N[i] :5);
End.
```

Output

Enter 5 Numbers
56
78
34
12
65

The Entered Numbers are
56   78   34   12   65

2. Searching an element in an Array

Ofcourse there are many algorithms available for searching an element in a linear array. We are confined to linear search. Initially, elements for an array were entered. Then search element required say, X should be entered. Now scanning starts from the first location to the end of the array. If the search element coincides with an array element then the control immediately come out of the loop after displaying the message "The Search number is found".If the search element is not found in the array, then the message "The Search number is not found" is displayed.

Here we are using the standard identifier "Exit" to come out of the loop, as it has been emphasized several times the importance of not using GOTO.

```
Program Example (Input,Output);
Var
             A: Array [1..10] of integer;
     I,Searchno, N: Integer;
Begin
     Writeln ('Enter How many Numbers do you want to enter ');
     Readln(n);
     Writeln('Enter ',N, 'Numbers ');
     For i:= 1 to n do
          Readln(A[i]);
     Writeln ('Enter Search Number ');
     Readln(Searchno);
     For i:= 1 to N do
          if (A[i] = Searchno) then
             begin
                Writeln ('The Search number is present ');
                Exit;
             end;
          Writeln('The Search Number is not present');
End.
```

Output

Enter How many Numbers do you want to enter
5
Enter 5 Numbers
456
123
987
543

Enter Search Number
987
The Search number is present

Enter How many Numbers do you want to enter
5
Enter 5 Numbers
100
200
300
400
500

Enter Search Number
150
The Search Number is not present

3. Inserting an element in an array

It is one of the important tasks in linear arrays, and the principle which we are going to adopt here will be discussed in detail in the latter part of this chapter.

At the start we should supply N elements for the array. Then an insertion position (P) and the value (V) should be fed. The algorithm behind this problem is as follows.

We have to move the last element to the location one above that. This process continues till the index reaches the position that we entered. Now we have the same element in the desired position and also in the index one above. At this stage the element which we want to insert is inserted at the current location. The elements below this position will not be perturbed. Finally we will have N+1 elements to display.

```
Program Example (Input, Output);
Var
            N : Array [1..10] of Integer;
         I,P,V,K : Integer;
Begin
    Writeln ('Enter How many numbers do you want to feed ');
    Readln (K);
    Writeln ('Enter' ,K, 'Numbers' );
    For i := 1 to k do
            Readln(N[i]);
```

```
Writeln( 'Enter Position to insert and its value);
Readln(P,V);
For i := K down to P do
        N[i+1] := N[i]; .
N[i] := V;
Writeln ('Elements in an array after insertion ');
For i:= 1 to k+1 do
        Writeln (N[i]);
End.
```

Output

Enter How many numbers do you want to feed
5
Enter 5 Numbers
456
123
987
45
Enter Position to insert and its value
3 345
Elements in an array after insertion
456
123
345
987
76
45

4. Deleting an element in an Array

In this case after entering 'n' elements for the array, it is enough that we feed the position (P) where we want to delete an element from the array. The detailed algorithm is given below for better understanding.

The elements in position P + 1 should be moved to the location P. Thus by decreasing one location for all elements till the index reaches total number of locations, we will have N − 1 elements to be displayed.

```
Program Example· (Input, Output);
Var
        N:Array[1..10] of Integer;
        I,P,K :Integer;
Begin
    Writeln ('Enter How many numbers do you want to feed );
```

```
Readln(K);
Writeln ('Enter' ,K, 'Numbers' );
For i := 1 to K do
        Readln(N[i]);
     Writeln ('Enter position to delete ');
Readln (P);
For i := P to K do
        N[i]:= N[i+1];
Writeln ('Elements in an array after deletion' );
For i := 1 to K -1 do
        Writeln (N[i]);
End.
```

Output

Enter How many numbers do you want to feed
5

Enter 5 numbers
87
98
112
45
67
Enter Position to delete
3
Elements in an array after deletion
87
98
45
67

Character Array

We are already familiar with the char, and now let us discuss the character array in much detail.

An array of character is called a "String". Suppose we want to store 10 names and each one having the maximum of 20 characters then the declaration for the above is as follows:

Var

StdNAME : ARRAY [1...10] Of String[20];

Here is an example which shows how character arrays can be handled. The example program is just to receive 5 name and to display entered 5 names.

```
Program Example (Input,Output);
Var
        name : Array [1..5] of String[20];
        i : integer;
Begin
        Writeln ('Enter 5 Names ');
        For i := 1 to 5 do
           Readln (Name[i]);
        Writeln( 'The Entered Names are ....');
        For i:= 1 to 5 do
           Writeln(Name[i]);
End.
```

Output

Enter 5 names
Dysan
Prinsel
Profile
Amkette
Maxell

The Entered Names are....
Dysan
Pinsel
Profile
Amkette
Maxell

Now we will see yet another example in which individual characters are accessed, though it is entered as a string. To illustrate the said process we are going to write a program to check whether the given word is a palindrome or not. (Palindrome is a sequence of characters that reads the same backward and forward. **MALAYALAM** is a palindrome)

```
Program Example(Input,output);
Var
        Givstr,Revstr ; String;
                I : Integer;
Begin
```

```
Writeln ('Enter String to Check' );
Readln(Givstr);
Revstr := '' ;
For i:= Length (Givstr) downto 1 do
    Revstr :=Revstr + Givstr[i];

if (Givstr = Revstr) then
  Writeln ('Given string is Palindrome')
else
    Writeln ('Given string is not a Palindrome');
End.
```

Output

Enter String to Check
malayalam
Given string is Palindrome

Enter String to check
Sivayavasi
Given string is not a Palindrome

Enter String to Check
able was i saw elba
Given string is Palindrome

Unlike **BASIC** where character in a string can be accessed only by using some of the built in functions (RIGHT$,MID$,LEFT$). here it is accessed by simply using its index (subscript).

Explanation about the Program.

Initially we have to pass a word to the program which we want to check. Then a second string is initialised with '' (Null). The only function used here is length, and the purpose of doing so is to find the length of the given string. Here 'For–Downto' loop is used from the length of the given string to 1 and the character relating to index is stored in the second string. Finally, after completing the loop the comparison takes place between the first string with the second one. If they were found to be equal then the entered string is palindrome otherwise it is not. From the above discussion it is seen that in Rascal, a character in a string can be accessed through its index.

Two-dimensional Array

We have already seen one–dimensional array in the previous section with suitable examples. In Turbo Pascal, we can have arrays more than one dimension, and the declaration of a two dimensional array takes the following form

VAR

ARRAY–NAME :ARRAY[LB..UB,LB..UB] of DATA–TYPE;

Here the data type may be integer, real, char or boolean.

For example the following declaration

VAR

A: ARRAY [1..3, 1..3] of INTEGER;

will reserve 9 memory location in the form of three rows and three columns, and it is represented as

A[1,1],   A[1,2],   A[1,3]

A[2,1],   A[2,2],   A[2,3]

A[3,1],   A[3,2],   A[3,3]

We may also call two dimensional array as a Table, since they store as table of values. Any element in the two dimensional array can be referred by giving the corresponding row subscript and column subscript.

Now let us consider the following example which illustrates how to receive elements for a two dimensional array and how to output the same.

```
Program Example(Input, Output);
Var
```

```
A : Array [1..3,1..3] of Integer;
I,J : Integer;
Begin
        Writeln ('Enter 9 Elements for A Matrix ');
        For i=1 to 3 do
          For j:= 1 to 3 do
            Readln(a[i,j]);
        Writeln('Output Matrix');
        For i:= 1 to 3 do
          begin
            For j:=1 to 3 do
              Write (A[i,j]:5);
            Writeln;
          end;
End.
```

Output

Enter 9 Elements for A Matrix
11
12
13
14
15
16
17
18
19

Output Matrix

```
   11   12   13
   14   15   16
   17   18   19
```

Explanation

For one dimensional arrays it is just enough to have only one subscript. Whereas in this case as we have already mentioned any element in a two dimensional array can be referenced by a row index followed by a column index. Here we have used **i** as the row index and j as the column index.

The above program receives values from the used in the following fashion,

```
A[1,1] ,        A[1,2] ,        A[1,3]
A[2,1] ,        A[2,2] ,        A[2,3]
A[3,1] ,        A[3,2] ,        A[3,3]
```

We may like to have the output of the matrix also in the above form. Again consider the following segment

```
For i:= 1 to 3 do
Begin
          For j:= 1 to 3 do
             Write (A[i,j]:4);
          WriteIn;
End;
```

Initially, the value of I and J are set to one. The program prints the values in the locations A[1,1], A[1,2] and A[1,3] in the same line as 'Write' is used to print the values. Next Writeln is used here to leave space in the current line and bring the pointer to next line. Thus we will get the matrix in the above form.

One fine example to illustrate the use of two dimensional array is matrix addition. In this program we have supplied nine elements for both A Matrix and B matrix. The resultant matrix C is obtained by using the following form

```
   C[i,j] := A[i,j]+ B[i,j];
```

here both i and j runs from 1 to 3

Here is a program to perform this task.

```
Program Example (Input,Output);
Var
          A,B,C : Array[1..3,1..3] of Integer;
          I,J : Integer;
Begin
          Writeln('Enter 9 Elements for A Matrix ');
          For i:= 1 to 3 do
            For j:= 1 to 3 do
              Readln (A[i,j]);

          Writeln('Enter 9 Elements for B Matrix ');
          For i:= 1 to 3 do
            For j:= 1 to 3 do
          Readln (B[i,j]);

          For i:= 1 to 3 do
          for j:= 1 to 3 do
```

```
            C[i,j]:= A[i,j]+B[i,j];

        Writeln ('The Output C matrix ');
        For i:= 1 to 3 do
            Begin
                For j:= 1 to 3 do
                Write (C[i,j]:5);
                Writeln;
            End;
End.
```

Output

Enter 9 Elements for A Matrix
1
2
3
4
5
6
7
8
9
Enter 9 Elements for B Matrix
1
2
3
4
5
6
7
8
9

The Output C matrix
```
  2    4    6
  8   10   12
 14   16   18
```

Here is another program for those who are not much familiar with mathematics. This program also illustrates all the fundamental array manipulations.

The fundamental array manipulations are

1. Sum all the elements

2. Row wise sum

3. Column wise sum

4. Sum of Main diagonal elements

5. Sum of off diagonal elements

Here is a program to perform all the above tasks.

```pascal
Program Example (Input, Output);
Var
        A : Array[1..3,1..3] of Integer;
        Allsum,I,J,Rowsum, Colsum,Diasum:Integer;
Begin
        Writeln ('Enter 9 Elements ');
        For i:= 1 to 3 do
            For j:= 1 to 3 do
                Readln (A[i,j]);
{Print the Given Elements} .
Writeln ('The Given Elements are ...');
   For i:= 1 to 3 do
      begin
           For j:= i to 3 do
              Write (A[i,j]:5);
           Writeln;
      End;

{Sum of all elements}
        Allsum:=0;
        For i:= 1 to 3 do
            For j:= 1 to 3 do
               Allsum := Allsum + A[i,j];
Writeln ('The Sum of All elements', Allsum);

{Sum Row wise}
        for i:= 1 to 3 do
            Begin
              Rowsum := 0;
                 For j := 1 to 3 do
                     Rowsum := Rowsum + A[i,j];
                Writeln('Row no : ' , I , .'Sum = ' ,Rowsum);
            End;
```

```
{Sum column wise}
        For i:= 1 to 3 do
          begin
            Colsum := 0;
            For j:= 1 to 3 do
              Colsum := Colsum + A[j,i];
              WriteIn('Column no :',I,'Sum =',Colsum);
          end;

{Sum main diagonal elements}
  Diasum := 0;
    For i:= 1 to 3 do
        Diasum := Diasum + A[i,i];
        Writeln ('Diagonal Sum ' , Diasum);

{Sum off diagonal elements}
  Diasum := 0;
    For i:= 1 to 3 do
        begin
          j := 4 -i,;
          Diasum := Diasum + A[i,j];
        end;
        Writeln ('Off Diagonal Sum ', Diasum);
End.
```

Output

Enter 9 Elements
33
12
21
56
64
78
99
43
19
The Given Elements are...
33   12   21
56   64   78
99   43   19

The Sum of All elements 425

Row no : 1 Sum = 66
Row no : 2 Sum = 198
Row no : 3 Sum = 161

Column no : 1 Sum = 188
Column no : 2 Sum = 119
Column no : 3 Sum = 118

Diagonal Sum 116
Off Diagonal Sum 184

Two-dimensional sorting

We can also have Two-dimensional sorting, and this is similar to one-dimensional sorting. A practical example which uses this technique is listed below.

```
Program Example (Input,Output);
Var
                  A : Array [1..20,1..20] of Integer;
    I,J,K,Temp,Order : Integer;
Begin'
     Writeln ('Enter Order of the Matrix ');
     Readln(Order);
     Writeln('Enter ',Order*Order,' elements 1 by 1');
      For i=1 to Order do
             For j:= 1 to order do
                 Readln(A[i,j]);

{Output the given matrix}
Writeln('The given matrix is ');
For i:= 1 to Order do
          begin
                For j:= 1 to order do
                Write (A[i,j]:5);
                Writeln;
          end;

{Sorting the number is columnwise}
For i:= 1 to order do
          For j:= 1 to order -1 do

             If a[j,i] > a[k,i] then
```

```
        For k:= J+1 to Order do
            begin
                Temp := A[j,i];
                A[j,i]:= A[k,i];
                A[k,i]:= Temp;
            end;
{Printing the Sorted matrix}
Writeln('Sorted Output Matrix ');
        For i:= 1 to Order do
            begin
                For j:= 1 to order do
                    Write(A[i,j]:5);
                Writeln;
            end;
End.
```

Output

Enter Order of the Matrix
3
Enter 9 elements 1 by 1
34
12
67
89
11
9
7
5
56
The given matrix is
34	12	67
89	11	9
7	5	56

Sorted Output matrix
7	5	9
34	11	56
89	12	67

In the above program we have confined to sort two-dimensional square matrix columnwise and the algorithmic approach is as follows:

1. Read the order of matrix

2. Read the elements of the matrix

3. Display the given matrix

4. Repeat step 5 to step 7 varying i from 1 by 1 until i > order

5. Repeat step 5 to step 7 varying j from 1 by 1 until j > order −1.

6. Repeat step 7 varying K from J + 1 by 1 until K > order

7. If A[j,i] > A[k,i] then interchange A[j,i], A[k,i]

8. Print the columnwise sorted matrix A

Multi-dimensional Arrays

Turbo Pascal allows more than two dimsensions. As the maximum number of dimension allowed varies from system to system, for the maximum dimensions one should refer to the Turbo Pascal manual. It is adviceable not to use more than three dimensions, as it occupies more memory space.

For example

Var

ABC : Array [1..10,1..10,1..10,1..10] of Integer;

Will occupy 10,000 locations in memory space.

In the following example we consider a case where there are 2 divisions in a departmental store Divn1, Divn2. Each division has 3 sections. The total sales of each section in a division is the sum of the sales of 5 days.

This is an example for a three dimensional array with

Two divisions

Three sections / division

Four days sales / section

```
Program Example (Input,output);
Var
        Sales : Array[1..2,1..3,1..4] of Integer;

        I,J,K,Divsale, Totsale, Secsale : LongInt;
Begin
        For I:= 1 to 2 do
```

```
Begin
    Writeln ('Sales for division ',i);
        For J:= 1 to 3 do
            begin
                Writeln ('Enter 4 days sales for section',j:3);
                    For K: 1 to 4 do
                        Readln(Sales[i;j,k]);
            end;
    End;
Totsale :=0;
    For I:= 1 to 2 do
    begin
        Divsale := 0;
        Writeln;
        Writeln('Division ',i);
        Writeln('Sec Sales');
        For J := 1 to 3 do
            begin
                Secsale := 0;
                For K := 1 to 4 do
                    Secsale := Secsale + Sales[i,j,k];
                Writeln(j:3,Secsale:7);
                Divsale :=Divsale + Secsale;
            end;
            Writeln('Total Sales in ',i,' Division ',divsale);
            Totsale := Totsale + Divsale;
    end;
    Writeln;
Writeln('Grand Total ', Totsale);
End.
```

Output

Sales for division 1
Enter 4 days sales for Section 1
1450
2980
450
6780
Enter 4 days sales for Section 2
4500
5200
1800
3450

Enter 4 days sales for Section 3
8790
10900
7650
3900
Sales for division 2

Enter 4 days sales for Section 1
3450
1890
2480
3250
Enter 4 days sales for Section 2
5600
8900
7560
9750
Enter 4 days sales for Section 3
9800
12100
8740
10100

Division 1
Sec Sales
1   11660
2   14950
3   31240
Total Sales in 1 division 57850

Division 2
Sec Sales
1   11070
2   31810
3   40740
Total Sales in 2 division 83620

Grand Total 141470

In the above sections we have discussed various forms of arrays, and their properties with suitable examples. The solved problems in the forthcoming pages will add new dimensions to the arrays.

Exercises

1. What is an array?

2. Write a program to find the smallest of a given set of numbers.

3. A typical element A_{ij} of a two dimensional array is the saddle point if A_{ij} is the smallest element in Row i and the largest element in Column j. Given matrix, write a PASCAL program to find a saddle point of the matrix, if one exist.

4. Write a program to find the second largest number in a given list of numbers and the position where they occur.

5. Write a program to arrange a given set of numbers in ascending order and descending order without writing two separate programs. Use CASE statement to perform the program.

6. Write a Pascal program to read a square matrix and to

   i) Check whether it is a symmetric matrix. A matrix is symmetric if $a_{ij} = a_{ji}$ for all values of i and j.

   ii) Find the norm of a matrix. The norm is defined as a square root of the sum of squares of all the elements in the matrix.

7. Write a program to read a set of quantities, count them and find the largest and the smallest quantities in the list. In addition, the program should count the number of quantities which are greater than 1000 and print all such quantities.

8. Write a program for processing examination marks. The output should give the list of

   i) Passed candidates and

   ii) Failed candidates

   (Assume that there are 5 papers and passing minimum is 40%)

9. Write a Pascal program to find the total number of +ve numbers, −ve numbers and zeros out of a set of 10 real numbers.

10. Write a program to find the volume of 10 different cylinders and to print out their radii, heights, volume in a serial order with a suitable heading.

11. Write a program which reads the names of three sales persons into a one-dimensional array and their sales figure in each of six months into a two dimensional array. The program then must print

the total sales for each sales person and the grand total for the six month as well.

12.   Write a Pascal program to find the mean, variance and standard deviation of a given set of numbers.

SOLVED PROBLEMS

1.   Write a program to generate Fibonacci series.

Fibonacci numbers is equal to the sum of the previous two, and it is given by

$$F_0 = 0$$

$$F_1 = 1$$

$$F_n = F_{n-1} + F_{n-2} \quad n > 1$$

Accept the number of rows to be printed as a result.

```
Program Example (Input,Output);
Var
        A : Array [1..100] of longint;
        N,I : Integer;
Begin
        Writeln('Enter How many terms do you want ');
        Readln(N);
        A[1]:=0;
        A[2] :=1;
        For I:= 3 to N do
        A[i] := A[i-1] + A[i-2];

    Writeln('The Fibonacci Series are ..');
        For i:= 1 to N do
        Write (A[i]:6);
End.
```

Output

Enter How many terms do you want
20
The Fibonacci Series are ..
        0 1 1 2 3 5   8 13   21   34   55   89   144
    233 377 610 987 1567 2584 4181

2. Write a program to find the number of numbers occur in the following range for a given 10 numbers.

Range 1 = 0–8

Range 2 = 9–15

Range 3 = > 15

```
Program Example (Input,Output);
Var
     A: Array[1..10] of Integer;
     R,R2,R3,I : Integer;
Begin
          Writeln ('Enter 10 elements');
          For i;= 1 to 10 do
               Readln(A[i]);
               R1 := 0; R2 := 0; R3 :=0;
          For i:= 1 to 10 do

               If (A[i] <= 8) then Inc (R1)
                    Else if (A[i] <=15) then Inc (R2)
          Else Inc(R3);

   Writeln ('No of elements less than 0-8 is = ',R1);
   Writeln ('No of elements fall between 9-15 is =',R2);
   Writeln ('No of elements greater than 15 is = ',R3);
End.
```

Output

Enter 10 elements
12
4
7
15
19
2
6
9
13
20

No of elements less than 0–8 is = 4
No of elements fall between 9–15 is = 4
No of elements greater than 15 is = 2

3. Write a program in PASCAL to print the PASCAL triangle given by

```
1
1   2   1
1   3   3   1
1   4   6   4   1
```

Accept the number of rows to be printed as result.

```
Program Example(Input,Output);
Var
         A: Array[1..10,1..10] of Integer;

    I,J,C,N: Integer;
Begin
         Writeln('Enter How many lines do you want ');
         Readln(N);
         A[1,1] := 1;
         Writeln(A[1,1]:5);
         A[2,1]:=1; A[2,2]:=2; A[2,3]:=1;
         Writeln(A[2,1]:5,A[2,2]:5,A[2,3]:5);
             For I := 3 to N do
             begin
             A[i,1]:= 1;
                Write(A[i,1]:5);
                J:=2; C:= 3;
                While (J <=I) do
                    begin
                        A[i,j] := A[i-1,c-1]+A[i-1,c-2];
                        Write(A[i,j]:5);
                        C:=c+1;
                        j:=j+1;
                    end;
                A[i,j]:=1;
                Writeln(A[i,j]:5);
             end;
End.
```

Output

Enter How many lines do you want
7

```
1
1    2    1
1    3    3    1
1    4    6    4    1
1    5   10   10    5    1
1    6   15   20   15    6    1
1    7   21   35   35   21    7    1
```

4.   Assume that there are two lists. List A contains **M** items and list B contains **N** items. The values of m and n are not necessarily identical. Write a program in pascal that merges all items of A and B into a single list C containing all elements of A and B.

```
Program Example (Input,Output);
Var
          A,B,C : Array [1..100] of Integer;
          M,N,I,S: Integer;
Begin
   Writeln('How many elements do you want to enter for array A');
   Readln(M);
   Writeln('Now enter ',M,' elements for array A');
   For I:= 1 to M do
      Readln(A[i]);

   Writeln('How many elements do you want to enter for array B');
   Readln(N);
   Writeln('Now enter ',N,' elements for array B');
   For I:= 1 to N do
      Readln(B[i]);


For I:= 1 to m do
          C[i]:= A[i];
S:=M;
For i:= 1 to N do
   begin
            S:=S+1;
          C[s]:=B[i];
   end;

Writeln('The Output list C contains, after merging ');
For i:= 1 to S do
   Write(C[i] :5);
End.
```

Output

How many elements do you want to enter for array A
4
Now enter 4 elements for array A
34
12
98
65
How many elements do you want to enter for array B
5
Now enter 5 elements for array B
76
54
123
86
24

The output list C contains, after merging
34 12 98 65 76 54 123 86 24

5.   Write a program to find Mode and its frequency.

```
Program Example(Input,Output);
Var
                A               : Array[1..100] of Integer;
  N,I,J,T,Freq,Max,Mode   : Integer;
Begin
    Writeln('Enter How many numbers Do you want to enter ');
    Readln(N);
    Writeln('Enter ',N,'Numbers ');
    For I :=1 to n do
          Readln(A[i]);

{Sorting the numbers by using bubble sort method}
          For I := 1 to N-1 do
            For J:= I+1 to N do
                If(A[i] <= A[j] ) then
                  begin
                    T := A[i]
                    A[i] := A[j];
                    A[j] := T;
                  end;
```

```
                {Finding the frequency of a number}
                Max := 0;
                For I := 1 to N-1 do
                If (A[i] <> A[i+1]) then
                    Freq := 0
                else If (A[i] = A[i+1]) then
                    Freq := Freq + 1;
                if (freq > max ) then
                        begin
                            Max := Freq:
                            Mode := A[i];
                        end;
Writeln('Mode : ',Mode);
Writeln('frequency : ',Max+1);
End.
```

Output

Enter How Many Numbers Do You Want To Enter
5
Enter 5 Numbers
4
6
4
9
4

Mode : 4

Frequency : 3

6. Write a program to copy the contents of an array called A into a
    array called B, Placing the numbers in the reverse order of whic
    they occupied in the original array. That is B(5) will contain A(1
    B(4) will contain A(2) etc.

```
Program Example (Input,Output);
Var
        A,B : Array [1..5] of Integer;
        I,J : Integer;
Begin
        Writeln('Enter 5 Elements ');
        For i:= 1 to 5 do
                Readln(A[i]);
```

```
            J:=1;
            For i:= 5 downto 1 do
            begin
               B[i] := A[j];
               J:= J+1;
            end;
Writeln ('After transferring elements ');
Writeln ('Location A B');
Writeln;
For i:= 1 to 5 do
     Writeln(i:4,A[i]:8,B[i]:8);
End.
```

Output

Enter 5 elements
78
65
49
98
45
After transferring elements
Location   A   B

1	78	45
2	65	98
3	49	49
4	98	65
5	45	78

7.   Let Name and Sex be two arrays that contain name and sex of
     the 5 members of a certain club. Male and Female are denoted
     by 'M' and 'F' respectively. Write a program which creates two new
     arrays, MALE and FEMALE such that MALE contains the names
     of all males and FEMALE contains the names of all the females.

```
Program Example(Input,Output);
Var
   Name,Male,Female : Array[1..10] of String;
                 Sex: Array[1..10] of String;
          NoM,NoF,I : Integer;
```

```
Begin
        For I:= 1 to 5 do
            Begin
                    Writeln('Enter Name');
                    Readln(Name[i]);
                    Writeln('Sex Code M /F ');
                    Readln(Sex[i]);
            End;
NoM:=0; NoF:=0;
          For i:= 1 to 5 do
            Begin
                If (Sex[i]='F') then
                     Begin
                        NoF             := NoF + 1 ;
                        Female[NoF]  := name[i];
                     End
                   Else
                     Begin
                        NoM             := NoM + 1;
                        Male[NoM]    := Name[I];
                     End;
            End;
Writeln('Number of ',NoM, ', Names are ..');
                For I := 1 to Nom do
                    Writeln(Male[i]);
                    Writeln;
Writeln('Number of Females ',NoF, ', Names are ..');
                For I := 1 to NoM do
                    Writeln (Female[i]);
End.
```

Output

Enter Name
Maxell
Sex Code M / F
M
Enter Name
Dysan
Sex Code M / F
F
Enter Name
Amkette

Sex Code M / F
M
Enter Name
Nipha
Sex Code M / F
F
Enter Name
Pinsel
Sex Code M / F
M
Number of Males 3 Names are ...
Maxell
Amkette
Pinsel
Number of Females 2 Names are ...
Dysan
Nipha

8.   Write a program to convert decimal to binary.

```
Program Example(Input,Output);
Var
     A : Array[1..20] of Integer;
N,I,J :Integer;

Begin
             Writeln(' Enter Number To Convert Binary ');
             Readln(N);
             I :=0;
             Repeat
               I:=I+1;
               A[i]:=N Mod 2;
               N:=trunc(n/2);
             Until (n <1);
Writeln (' Output in Binary form is .. ');
     For J:= I Downto 1 do
           Write (A[j]);
End.
```

Output

Enter Number To Convert Binary
65
Output in Binary form is..
1000001

(Hint. Here Integer Function Trunc( ) is to round the real number. For example if x=2.4 then after truncation it gives 2 and if x = 3.5 it gives 3)

9. Two sets of data relating to 100 persons, namely age [100], and income [100] are available (both integer arrays). Write a program to compute the average income of person aged between 25 years and 30 years (both inclusive).

```pascal
Program Example (Input,Output);
Var
      Age,Income : Array[1..5] of Integer ;
      No,I,TotInc : Integer;
      AveInc : Real :
Begin
      Writeln ('Enter Age, income for 5 persons 1 by 1 ');
      TotInc := 0 ;
      No := 0;
      For I:= 1 to 5 do
              If (Age[i] >= 25) And (Age[i] <=30) then
                  Begin
                      TotInc := TotInc + Income[i]:
                      No := No + 1;
                  End;
AveInc := TotInc / No ;
Writeln ('Average income For Age between 25-30 is ', AveInc :7:2);
End.
```

Output

Enter Age, Income for 5 Persons 1 by 1
18 1250
27 2000
31 4500
29 7800
30 5600

Average Income For Age Between 25–30 is 5133.33

10. Write a Pascal program to alphabetize the given 5 names

OR

Develop a Pascal program that would sort and display a given arbitrary array of names in the ascending order.

```
Program Example (Input,Output);
Var
      Name : Array[1..5] of string;
      Temp : String;
      I,J : Integer ;
Begin
      Writeln ('Enter 5 Names 1 by 1');
      For I := 1 to 5 do
            Readln (Name[i]);

      For I := 1 to 4 do
              For J := i+1 to 5 do
                  If (Name[i] > Name[j]) then
                      Begin
                          Temp   := Name[i] ;
                          Name[i] := Name[j] ;
                          Name[j] := Temp;
                      End;
Writeln( 'Sorted names are ...');
For    I := 1 to 5 do
   Writeln(Name[i]);
End.
```

Output

Enter 5 Names 1 by 1
Pascal
Lisp
Cobol
Ada
Basic
Sorted Names are ...
Ada
Basic
Cobol
Lisp
Pascal

11. Write a program to exchange the contents of two arrays.

```
Program Example(Input,Output);
Var
   A,B,T : ARRAY [1..5] of Integer;
   I : Integer ;
Begin
          Writeln('Enter 5 Elements for Array A ');
          For I := 1 to 5 do
             Readln(A[i]);
          Writeln('Enter 5 Elements for Array B ');
          For I := 1 to 5 do
          Readln(B[i]);
          {Swaping}
          T:=A;
          A:=B;
          B:=T;
          Writeln('The Elements in Array A After Swaping ');
          For I:= 1 to 5 do
          Write(A[i]:5);
          Writeln;
          Writeln('The Elements in Array B after Swaping ');
                 For I:= 1 to 5 do
                    Write(B[i]:5);
End.
```

Output

Enter 5 Elements for Array A
23
45
67
89
34

Enter 5 Elements for Array B
65
74
82
90
123

The Elements in Array A after Swaping
    65   74   82   90   123
The Elements in Array B after Swaping
    23   45   97   89   34

12. Write a Program to convert Two dimensional into One dimensional Array

```
Program Example(Input,Output);
Var
     A : Array [1..3,1..3] of integer ;
     B : Array [1..9] of integer;
K,I,J : Integer ;
Begin
   Writeln('Enter 9 elements 1 by 1');
   For I:= 1 to 3 do
    ' For J:= 1 to 3 do
      Readln(A[I,J]);

   K:=0;
     For I:= 1 to 3 do
      For J:= 1 to 3 do
        Begin
            K  := K+1;
            B[K]  := A[I,J];
        End;

Writeln('Output in one dimension');

For i:=1 to 9 do
. Write(B[i]:3);
Writeln;

End.
```

Output

Enter 9 elements 1 by 1
4
6
8
9
2
*5
'9
7
1
Output in one dimension
4 6 8 9 2 5 9 7 1

CHAPTER - 6

PROCEDURES AND FUNCTIONS

Every language has its own features and properties. For example, in BASIC it is line numbers. In FORTRAN it is Format statements and in COBOL it is divisions. Similarly there is no Pascal without Procedures.

Programs are classified into two. One is the main program, and it is one which executes by itself i.e. without expecting any help from any other source. The other is the sub-program, which executes only from the main program. Eventhough a sub-program has almost all the features of the main program, it cannot execute independently and it has to execute only from the main program. Here we call such a sub-program as Modules. One of the property of a structured programming aspect is to break a large program into several individual modules, to enable the user to scan the program and to remove errors easily.

Advantage of Using Sub-Programs

There are occasions where we may want to do a particular action repetitively in a program. If we code it repeatedly in our main program it will not look nice, and the program may also become too lengthy. Suppose in one of our program we want to find the area of a triangle for different sets of values, it is not possible for us to code the program wherever it was warranted. Developing one such sub-program, we can call this wherever necessary by supplying suitable values.

This feature can be used in the development of large programs where separate sub-programs of the large program need to be developed individually.

In this Chapter, we will see how to use Procedures and Functions effectively. In addition to that we will see the difference between the Procedures and Functions. Now let us plunge into Procedures which make Pascal, a glorified language in the spectrum of computer language.

PROCEDURES

There are two general format available for procedures, and the first one is

```
Procedure Proc.name;
Label ;
const ;
Var ;
```

```
Procedure ;
function ;
begin
   statements ;
end;
```

By using the above prototype let us write a procedure to display a message 'Welcome'

```
Procedure Wel ;
begin
   Writeln ('Welcome') ;
end;
```

Now there are two questions in front of us. One is that where can we place this procedure? and another is how can we invoke this procedure?. The structure of Pascal comes to rescue us in this stage. We have seen that Procedure or Function, if any, should be defined before the beginning of the main program. Thus, our Program turns into the following form :

```
Program Example (Input, Output);
Var
    I : Integer;
Procedure Wel;
begin
        Writeln ('Welcome');
end;
{Main Starts}
begin
        For I = 1 to 5 do
           Wel;

end
```

Output

Welcome
Welcome
Welcome
Welcome
Welcome

To invoke the procedure it is just enough to mention the name of the procedure where it is necessary. On encountering this, the control is transferred to the procedure part. After executing the Procedure, control returns to the next statement following the Procedure name.

Now let us see another program to find the cube of a given number, to understand the concept of procedure still better.

```
Program Example (Input, Output);
Var                    .
          N : Integer;
Procedure Cube;
Var
          X : Integer;
begin
          X : = N * N * N;
          Writeln ('The cube of the given number is ',x);
end;
{Main Starts}
begin
          Writeln ('Enter number to find cube');
          Readln(N);
          Cube;
end.
```

Output

Enter number to find cube
4
The cube of the given number is 64
Enter number to find cube
23
The cube of the given number is 12167

Initially we have to feed the value of N for which we need to calculate the cube value. We invoke the Procedure Cube. As N is declared outside of this procedure, the value of N is retained in the procedure. So, after printing the cube of a given number the program comes to an end.

Global Variables and Local Variables

In the above program, we have used the value of N in the procedure without any declaration in the procedure. Such a variable is called a global variable. It is defined as a variable which is declared outside of any procedure or function. The scope of those variables is throughout the program so that we can make use of those variables without redefining in any procedure or function. On the contrary the variables declared inside of any procedure or function are said to be local variables.

The values of these variables ceases immediately when we come out of the procedure.

Passing Parameter to a Procedure

In the above two examples we are passing variables to procedures by declaring them as global ones. There is yet another way in which we can pass variables. Here we pass the variables along with the procedure call. The purpose of doing so is to make our procedure, not specific (generic) to a particular program, where the variables are declared as global variables. This can be achieved by using a second form of the procedure.

The general format is

```
Procedure Proc.name(var list and its type);
Label ;
Const ;
Var ;
Procedure ;
Function ;
begin
   Statements;
end;
```

Now we will rewrite the previous example by passing the variables to the procedure, along with the Procedure call.

```
Program Example (Input, Output);
Var
                N : Integer;
Procedure Cube (Y : Integer);
Var
            X : Integer;
  begin
            X : =Y * Y * Y;
        Writeln ('The cube of the given number is ',X)
  end;
{Main Starts}
begin
            Writeln('Enter number to find cube ');
            Readln (N)
            cube (N)
end.
```

Output

Enter number to find cube
5
The cube of the given number is 125
Enter number to find cube
98
The cube of the given number is 23688

Here, after receiving the value for N, the **Procedure Cube** is invoked along with the variable N. The value of N is transferred to Y by the Procedure declaration. Thus we can pass the value of N to Y in this way. The variables in the procedure call are called as actual parameters and the variable in the procedure declaration are called as formal parameters.

Now, consider the following example where the same variable is declared in the main, as well as in the procedure.

```
Program Example(Input,Output);
Var
          X : Integer;
Procedure Test(Y :Integer);
Var
          X : Integer;
Begin
  X :=9;
  Writeln('The Value of x inside the Procedure is ',x );
  Y := Y * X ;
  Writeln('The Value of X * Y is ',Y);
End;
{ Main Starts}
Begin
  X := 5;
  Writeln('The Value of X in Main is ', X);
  Test(X);
  Writeln('The Value of X in Main after executing procedure is ', X);
End.
```

Output

The Value of X in Main is 5
The Value of X inside the Procedure is 9

The Value of X * Y is 45
The Value of X in Main after executing procedure is 5

Here **X** is declared in the main and it is defined as 5. The value of X is transferred to the procedure where again, **X** is declared as local variable. Inside the procedure, X is initialised as 9 and it is used to multiply **Y**. Thus the above example vividly explains that if the same identifier is declared both in the main and in the procedure, the procedure considers only the local variable. When the procedure is completed the value as defined in the main will come in to being.

Parameter Communication Between Procedure and Main

Let us have a closer look over the communication of parameters between a Procedure and the main.

There are two modes of transferring variables between procedure and main and they are

1. Value Parameter
2. Variable Parameter

We will see the above two types with suitable examples one by one.

Value Parameter

In this mode of communication, only the values of actual parameters of the Procedure call are transferred to the formal parameters of procedure declaration. So, changes taking place inside the procedure will not affect the corresponding parameters in the procedure call. Hence this way of communication is also called as "Call by Value".

The following example will illustrate the above principle.

```
Program Example(Input,Output);
Var
        A,B,C : Integer;
Procedure Test(X,Y,Z : Integer);
Begin
  X := X * X ; Y := Y * Y ; Z := Z * Z;
  Writeln('The Values of A,B,C in Procedure is ',X:4,Y:4,Z:4);
End;
{ Main Starts }
Begin
  Writeln('Enter 3 Values ');
  Readln(A,B,C);
  Writeln('The Values of A,B,C before entering Procedure is',A:4,B:4,C:4);
  Test(A,B,C);
```

```
   Writeln('The Values of A,B,C after executing Procedure is ',A:4,B:4,C:4);
End.
```

Output

Enter 3 Values
4 5 6
The Values of A,B,C before entering Procedure is 4 5 6
The Values of A,B,C in Procedure is 16 25 36
The Values of A,B,C after executing Procedure is 4 5 6

Variable Parameter

In this mode, not only the value of the actual parameter of the procedure call is passed to the formal parameter of procedure declaration but also the variable reference. If any changes take place inside the procedure, it will automatically influence the corresponding variables in the procedure call. So, it is also called as a "Variable Parameter". This effect can be achieved simply by adding **Var** before any formal parameters in the procedure declaration. The example program follows to fulfill the above idea.

```
Program Example(Input,Output);
Var
         A,B,C : Integer;
Procedure Test(Var X,Y,Z : Integer);
Begin
   X := X * X ; Y := Y * Y ; Z := Z * Z;
   Writeln('The Values of A,B,C in Procedure is ' ,X:4,Y:4,Z:4);
End;
{ Main Starts }
Begin
   Writeln('Enter 3 Values ');
   Readln(A,B,C);
   Writeln('The Values of A,B,C before entering Procedure is',A:4,B:4,C:4);
   Test(A,B,C);
   Writeln('The Values of A,B,C after executing Procedure is ',A:4,B:4,C:4);
End.
```

Output

Enter 3 Values
4 5 6
The Values of A,B,C before entering Procedure is 4 5 6

The Values of A,B,C in Procedure is 16 25 36
The Values of A,B,C after executing Procedure is 16 25 36

From the above two examples it is seen that in the Value Parameter the value before and after executing the procedure remains the same and it changes only inside the procedure. In **Variable Parameter**, the values inside the Procedure is same even after executing the procedure.

The choice of using the above techniques is left with the programmers, and the choice may be depending on the requirement of the programs. If we want to pass just the value of parameters to the Procedures, value parameters are enough. If we need any change to be done inside the procedures, then Variable parameters are preferred.

From the above two cases it is clear that in the Procedure the transfer of value between Procedure and Main is only through its Parameters.

Let us see some tips and tricks.

Consider the following Procedure declaration.

```
Procedure Biggest( X,Y,Z : Integer);
```

then the Procedure call may be either of the following two ways.

```
Biggest(A,B,C);
or
Biggest(10,20,30);
```

In both cases, these values are transferred to the Procedure and the Procedure returns the correct result for which it is intended.

Now consider the second way of Procedure declaration

```
Procedure Biggest ( Var X,Y,Z : Integer );
```

In this case the Procedure Call should definitely be

```
Biggest (A,B,C) ;
```

It is because, in the above Procedure the formal parameters are declared as Variable Parameters, which returns the final result of the formal parameter in the Procedure to the main program. So, it is essential that to pass a result to the main, there should be variables in the Procedure call statement.

From the above two cases it is immaculate that Procedure call can have either constant or variable as an actual parameter provided that the formal parameters are not variable parameters. Whereas there should be variables when the formal parameters are of variable type.

It is also evident that variables are the only nexus between Procedures and the main Program.

Passing an array to a Procedure

Similar to passing an element to a procedure we can also transfer entire arrays to a procedure.

For example to pass an array A which is having 5 integer elements to the procedure Max, the procedure call might look like

```
Max(A);
```

To pass an array, it is enough to refer the name of the array along with the procedure call.

Consider the following call

```
Max(A[10]);
```

In the above call only the value of A[10] is passed to the Procedure Max and not an the entire array.

Let us see how a Procedure declaration might look when it is used to receive an array.

Consider the following invalid declaration.

```
Procedure Max( X : array [1..10] of Integer);
```

It is so because, in Procedure declaration only simple data types should be passed and not structured data types.

A type declaration statement may also be used to transfer arrays to a Procedure.

Consider the declaration

```
Type
W = Array [1..10] of Integer;
```

In the above declaration **W** is a user defined type to denote an array of

10 integer elements. So, whenever we want to declare an array of 10 integer elements the user defined type W is used in variable declaration as shown below :

```
Type
     W = Array[1..10] of Integer ;
Var
     A : W ;
```

The above declaration is same as

```
Var
     A : Array[1..10] of Integer;
```

Now we can use this same method to the Procedure declaration also and the correct form of Procedure declaration is

```
Procedure Sort Array ( X : W);
```

Where W is the user defined data type for Array type and it is declared before the variable declaration.

Let us get more used to this technique through a practical example illustrated below:

Program to Sort the given 5 numbers using Procedure.

```
Program Example (Input, Output);
Type
     W = Array[1..5] of Integer ;
Var
     A : W ;
     I : Integer;
Procedure SortArray ( Var X : W ) ;
Var
     I,J,T : Integer ;
Begin
          For I := 1 to 4 do
               For J := i+1 to 5 do
                    If ( X[i] > X[j] ) then
                         Begin
                              T := X[i];
```

```
                        X[i] := X(j);
                        X[j] := T;
                  End;
End;
{ Main Starts }
Begin
        Writeln('Enter 5 Numbers 1 by 1 ')
        For I := 1 to 5 do
           Readln(A[i]);
        SortArray(A);
        Writeln('Sorted Array Contains ... ');
        For I := 1 to 5 do
           Writeln(A[i]);
End.
```

Output

Enter 5 Numbers 1 by 1
34
56
12
33
98
Sorted Array Contains ...
12
33
34
56
98

Explanation

Initially the user has to enter 5 numbers, which he wants to sort in the array. Then the procedure call SortArray(A) will transfer the entire array to the Procedure SortArray. In the Procedure declaration array X is declared as a variable parameter, the changes will be transferred to array A in main program. The array gets sorted by using the method which we have seen already in the previous chapter. Finally, the sorted array X is transferred to A of the procedure call.

Procedure Within Procedure

As seen from the general form of the Procedure any number of Procedures can be included within a procedure.

The following program will illustrate how one procedure can be included within another procedure.

```
Program Example (Input, Output);
Type
          W = Array[1..5] of Integer ;
Var
          A : W ;
          I : Integer ;
Procedure SortArray (Var X : W) ;
Var
          I,J : Integer ;
Procedure Swap (Var P,Q : Integer) ;
Var
          T : Integer;
Begin
          T : = P ;
          P : = Q ;
          Q : = T ;
End;
{Procedure SortArray Starts}
Begin
          For I := 1 to 4 do
            For J := I+1 to 5 do
               If (X[I] > X [J]) then
                  Swap (X[I], X[J]);
End;

{Main Starts}
Begin
          Writeln('Enter 5 Numbers 1 by 1');
          For I := 1 to 5 do
            Readln(A[I]);
          SortArray(A);
          Writeln('Sorted Array Contains ...');
          For I := 1 to 5 do
            Writeln (A[I]);
End.
```

Output

Enter 5 Numbers 1 by 1

34
56
123
44
98
Sorted Array Contains ...
34
44
56
98
123

Explanation

The above example program is same as the previous one except that in Procedure SortArray we have used another Procedure Swap to exchange the values between the variables. Procedure Swap uses the variable Parameters P and Q so that the resultant would affect the actual Parameters **X[i]** and **X[j]**. Thus procedures can also be nested by using the above method.

In the above sections we have discussed various forms of procedures, their properties etc. Let us have our discussion through more elaborated problems in the solved problem section.

Functions

It has been mentioned earlier that one main advantage and strong factor of Pascal is the use of procedure and function. The Pascal functions can be divided into Library functions or Built in functions and user defined functions. The difference between these two is that library functions are built functions. These are not developed by the user. On the other hand a user defined function has to be developed by the user. The Pascal functions are not only very easy but also very versatile. In the previous section, procedures were used to return one value or more than one value to the main. But functions should be used to return only one value to main. This is where procedure and function differ from one another. In this section, we shall discuss how function is defined and how to use them along with the main program to make Pascal program as a more structured one. We will be discussing about library functions later in this chapter.

The simplest form of the user defined function is

```
Function Function. Name (Var list) : Data type;
Const;
```

```
Var;
Begin
     statements ;
     Function.name := result;
End;
```

Function is a reserved word and function name is an identifier given by the user followed by formal parameters and their types. As we have already observed that function return only one value. We know the data type of the value it returns. This should also be given along with the declaration. Inside the function usual declaration like Const and Var followed by a group of statements enclosed by Begin and End must be given.

Let us write a simple function to calculate the area of the triangle.

Formula to compute the area of a triangle is

Area = 22/7 * Base * Height

```
Function Area (Base, Height : Real) : Real ;
Begin
     Area := 0.5 * Base * Height ;
End;
```

The function name is **Area**. Formal parameters are separated by a comma that receive the values when the function is called from main program.

Inside the function, the computed value is assigned to a function name Area. The important point to be noted here is that value from the function returns only through the name of the function. Here again procedure deviates, where the communication between main and procedure are through arguments only. In the case of functions after receiving a value to the function name it returns to the main where it is used.

Now we will complete a program by incorporating the above function

```
Program Example (Input, Output);
Var
          B,H,TriArea : Real ;
Function Area (Base, Height : Real) : Real ;
Begin
          Area : = 0.5 * Base * Height ;
End;
```

```
{ Main Starts }
Begin
        Writeln('Enter Base, Height');
        Readln(B,H);
        TriArea : = Area(B,H);
        Writeln('Area of a Triangle is ',TriArea:8:2);
End.
```

Output

Enter Base, Height

45 78

Area of a Triangle is 1755.00

Explanation

Here **Base** and **Height** receive their values through the identifiers B, H respectively. Then the function **Area** is called along with the received arguments B and H, and the returned value is assigned to TriArea and it is displayed.

In the above program function is called through an assignment statement. It is also referenced by any one of the following ways.

i. As a part of an output statement

e.g.

```
        Writeln('Area of a Triangle is ',Triarea(B,H) : 8:2)
```

ii. As a part of an expression

e.g.

```
        Totarea := Triarea(B,H) * 12;
```

iii. As a part of a comparison

e.g.

```
        If (TriArea(B,H) > 100) then
                Writeln ('Area is too high');
```

Thus the function can be invoked by using any one of the above methods.

Let us have a closer look over the function by coding another program using a Function.

Program to find Binomial Coefficient using the formula

$N_c R = N ! / R ! * (N - R) !$

```
Program Example (Input, Output);
Var
        N,R : Integer;
        Bino : Real;
Function Fact (X : Integer) : Integer;
Var
        I,Prod : Integer;
Begin
        Prod : = 1;
        For I : = 1 to X do
          Prod : = Prod * I;
        Fact : = Prod;
End;
{Main Starts}
Begin
        Writeln('Enter Values for N, R');
        Readln (N,R);
        Bino : = Fact (N) / Fact (R) * Fact (N - R) );
        Writeln ('Binomial Coefficient ',Bino:8:2);
End.
```

Output

Enter Values for N, R
5 3
Binomial Coefficient 10.00

Explanation

Initially we have to key in the values for N and R for which we want to find out the Binomial coefficient. Then by making use of these variables, function Fact with N is called first. Thus the value of the actual parameter N is transferred to the formal parameter X of the function declaration.

Upon scanning the function, one (FORTRAN programmers) might ask why do we use a temporary identifier (Prod) instead of using **Fact** directly. As we have said earlier that the value of the function returns only through its name and it should not be initialised more than once, we are in need of temporary variable to find the result and it is assigned to function name before the function ceases. So, in every function, the function name should appear atleast once in the left hand side of an assignment statement, whereas in the case of procedure it is not necessary.

Functions with Arrays

So far we have been discussing about passing values of variables to function. It is also possible to pass the values of an array to function, the process is similar to that in the case of procedures.

For example the function call

```
Max = Biggest(A)
```

Will pass all the elements in the array to function Biggest, and the function declaration of the same would be

```
Function Biggest (X : W) : Integer;
```

Where **W** is the user defined data type for an array of 10 Integer quantities. As structured data types are not permitted in the function declaration, the property is identical as in procedure. An example program is given below.

```
Program Example (Input, Output);
Type
        W = Array [1..5] of Integer;
Var
        A : W;
        I, Max : Integer;
Function Biggest (X : W) : Integer;
Var
        I,M : Integer;
Begin
        M := X[1];
        For I := 2 to 5 do
        If (M < X[I]) then M := X[I];
        Biggest := M;
End;
```

```
{Main Starts}
Begin
        Writeln('Enter 5 Numbers 1 by 1');
        For I := 1 to 5 do
        Readln(A[i]);
        Max := Biggest(A);
        Writeln('The Maximum No is ',Max);
End.
```

Output

Enter 5 Numbers 1 by 1
45
123
98
76
54
The Maximum No is 123

Explanation

Initially the user has to enter the numbers among with he wants to find the maximum, as the given array. Then the statement

```
Max : =Biggest (A)
```

will transfer all these elements of the array A to the function Biggest. In function Biggest, the maximum number is obtained by using the method which we have already seen in the previous chapter (Arrays). The value of Biggest is returned to the main and the same is displayed.

The examples so far have shown how to use function to return numeric values. Sometime you may just want to know whether the entered array of elements are in an ascending order or not. To perform this we have used function which return boolean as its value i.e. True or False in the following program.

```
Program Example (Input, Output);
Type
        W = Array[1..5] of Integer;
Var
        X : W;
        I : Integer;
Function AscOrder(A : W) : Boolean;
Var
```

```
            Check : Boolean;
            I : Integer ;
Begin
            Check := True ;
            I:= 1;
            While ( (I < 5) and (Check)) do
               Begin
                  If (A[i] > A[i+1]) Then Check := False;
                  i:= i + 1 ;
               End;
            AscOrder := Check ;
End;

{ Main Starts }
Begin
         Writeln('Enter 5 Numbers 1 by 1 ');
         For i:= 1 to 5 do
            Readln(X[i]);
         If (AscOrder(X)) Then
            Writeln('Given Numbers are in Ascending Order ' )
         else
            Writeln('Given Numbers are not in Ascending Order ' );
End.
```

Output

Enter 5 Numbers 1 by 1
23
45
87
98
123
Given Numbers are in Ascending Order
Enter 5 Numbers 1 by 1
87
65
99
110
123
Given Numbers are not in Ascending Order

Explanation

After getting the values for the array X, the elements are transferred to function **AscOrder**. Inside the function, boolean variable **Check** is initialised to True and it is used to find whether the element in the array are in an order. Index starts from 1 and it is compared with the value in the next location. If the first location value is greater than the second location the boolean variable Check takes its value as False, and the loop terminates. If not the index goes upto 4 so as to compare with the next one. Finally after completing the comparison **Check**, it is assigned to the function name **AscOrder**, which is used as a part of the comparison statement in main. If it evaluates to True, then the entered numbers are in ascending order, if not they are not in proper order.

Library Functions

Pascal is enriched with many built in functions to cater to the needs of scientific and graphic fields. Let us see some of its important built in functions category wise.

I. NUMERIC FUNCTIONS

a. Abs(x)

To find the absolute value of x, where x may be real or integer. If the value of x is less than 0 then Abs(x) changes the sign of x and displays the value of x.

```
x := 5.6;                    x : =-6.7;
Writeln(Abs(x):5:2);     Writeln(Abs(x):5:2);
```

Output

5.6   6.7

b. Arctan(x)

To find the trigonometric arctangent of x , value of x may be either integer or real but it is expressed in radians.

c. Cos(x)

To find the cosine of x. Here also x may be an integer or a real and it is expressed in radians. For example to find cos (45) the following program segment may be used.

```
Degree:=45;
Radian:=3.14/180*Degree;
Writeln(Cos(Radian):8:3);
```

Output

0.707

d. Exp(x)

To find the exponent value of x. It is inverse of Ln(x) function. The value of E is 2.718282. Here x may be real or integer.

For example

Exp(3) is equal to 2.718282³

e. Frac(x)

To extract the fractional part from the real value(x).

For example

```
x:=34.567;
Writeln(Frac(x));
```

will return

0.567

f. Int(x)

It is used to return the integral part of x. The result is always integer.

For example

```
x:=87.99;
Writeln(Int(x):8:3);
```

will return

87.000

g. Ln(x)

To find the natural logarithm of base e. Here x may be real or integer and it is the inverse of Ln(x).

For example

To compute natural logarithm (base e)

To compute natural logarithm (base 10)

```
x := 20;                    x := 20;
Writeln(Ln(x):8:3);         Writeln(Ln(x)/Ln(10):8:3);
```

will return

2.996   1.301

h. Pi

It is used to return the value of Π

```
        Writeln(Pi:8:3);
```

will return

3.142

i. Random

It is one of the functions which does not have any arguments. It is used to return a value which lies between 0 and 1, hence the result is always real.

j. Random(x)

Here x must be an integer value which lies between 0 to 65535. This function returns an integer less than x.

k. Sin(x)

To find the sine of x. Here x may be integer or real and it is expressed in radians. For example to find Sin(45) the following program segment may be used.

```
Degree:=45;
Radian:=3.14/180*Degree;
Writeln(Sin(Radian):8:3);
```

will return

0.707

l. Sqr(x)

To find the square of x where x may be real or integer

m. Sqrt(x)

To find the square root of x where x may be real or integer.

n. Round(x)

It is used to convert real value(x) to an integer by rounding, x must be real and the result is an integer.

```
x:=98.5;
Writeln(Round(x));
```

will return

99

o. Trunc(x)

It is used to convert a real value to an integer by eliminating the decimal part. Here x must be real.

```
x:=98.5;
Writeln(Trunc(x));
```

will return

98

The above two functions are used to return only Integer values.

II. STRING FUNCTIONS

Next to BASIC, Turbo Pascal is well equipped with numerous String Functions and String Procedures and these functions and procedures are very easy and are ready to use.

String Functions

a. Contact (Str1, Str2, ..., StrN) :

This function is used to add any number of strings Str1, Str2, Str3, etc. The general form is

ResultantString : = Concat (Str1, Str2,....., StrN)

(e.g.)

```
Program Example (Input, Output);
Var
          , Str1, Str2, Str3, Str4 : String;
Begin
```

```
            Str1 := 'God';
            Str2 := 'Bless';
            Str3 := 'You';
            Str4 := Concat (Str1, Str2, Str3);
            Writeln(Str4);
            Readln;
End.
```

Output

God Bless You

The same could also be achieved by the following program without using the Concat( ) function.

```
            Str4 := Str1 + Str2 + Str3;
```

and the Output is

God Bless You

Concat means linking. Thus we can link strings to form a resultant string.

b. Copy (SourceStr, StartingPoint, NoOfChars) :

The counterpart for the above function in Basic is Mid$. It is used to extract a string from another string, provided that the starting point of the string and the number of characters to be extracted from that point are given. The general form is

```
ResultantString:=Copy(SourceStr,StartingPoint,NoOfChars);
```

(e.g.)

```
Program Example (Input, Output);
Var
        SourceString, ResultantString: string;
begin
        SourceString := 'Cray XMP-14';
        ResultantString := copy (SourceString,6,3,);
        Writeln(ResultantString);
end.
```

Output

XMP

Starting from the 5th character three characters of the source string are printed.

By implicit the above two functions return string values.

Next we will see the String Functions which return an integer value.

c. Length(Str) :

The above string is used to count the number of characters given in the string.

The general form is

```
Len := Length(Str);
```

(e.g.)

```
Program Example (Input, Output);
Var
        Str:string;
        Len:integer;
begin
        Str := 'Nikalus Wirth';
        Len := Length(Str);
        Writeln(Len);
end.
```

Output

13

d. Pos(PatternStr, SourceStr) :

If pattern string appears within source string, the function returns the position of the first character of the match. The function returns zero, if no match is found.

The general form is

```
Locn := Pos (PatternStr, SourceStr);
```

e.g.)

```
Program Example (Input, Output);
Var
        PatternStr, SourceStr:string;
        Locn:integer;
begin
        PatternStr := 'Perfect';
        SourceStr := 'Be Perfect and Sincere';
        Locn := Pos(PatternStr, SourceStr);
        Writeln(Locn);
end.
```

Output

4

String Procedures

Turbo Pascal has some of the unique string procedures which make string manipulation very easier than in other languages.

a. Inser (SourceStr, DestinationStr, Position) :

This procedure allows us to insert a Source string into a Destination string at a desired location (Position).

SourceStr   Source String Specifying the string to insert

DestinationStr   Destination String where the insertion takes place

Position   An integer denotes the character position in destination
                 where the insertion begins.

```
Program Example (Input, Output);
Var
        SourceStr, DestinationStr : string;
        Position:integer;
begin
        SourceStr := 'Love';
        DestinationStr := 'I India':
        Position := 3;
        Insert (SourceStr, DestinationStr, Position);
        Writeln(DestinationStr);
end.
```

Output

I Love India

b. Delete (DestinationStr, Position, NoOfChars) :

This procedure eliminates a substring from another string. The deletion begins at Position of the Destination string and it stops only after eliminating NoOfChars. Thus the length of resulting string (DestinationStr) is less than the original string.

DestinationStr   The string where the deletion takes place

Position   An integer denotes the character position in destination where the deletion begins

NoOfChars   An integer representing the number of characters to delete from the DestinationStr

(e.g.)

```
Program Example (Input, Output)
Var
        DestinationStr:string;
        Position, NoOfChars:integer;
begin
        DestinationStr := 'Turbo 2000 Plus';
        Position := 7;
        NoOfChars := 5;
        Delete (DestinationStr, Position, NoOfChars);
        Writeln(DestinationStr);
end.
```

Output

Turbo Plus

c. Val(StringValue, NumericVariable, ErrorCode) :

There are occasions where we may get a numeric value in the form of string. If in the same program we want to convert this string into numeric value, we can use this procedure Val.

StringValue   A String but consists only numerals

NumericVariable   This may be either real or integer variable. The string is converted to a number and it is stored in Numeric Variable.

ErrorCode   While in conversion if any error occurs ErrorCode contains the position of the error within the string.

If there is no error, the value of ErrorCode is 0. ErrorCode is an integer variable.

(e.g.)

```
Program Example (Input, Output);
Var
        ErrorCode : Integer;
        StringValue : string;
        NumVar : Real;
begin
        StringValue : = '2346.78';
        Val(StringValue, NumVar, ErrorCode);
        Writeln(NumVar:8:2)
end.
```

Output

2346.78

d. Str (NumericValue, StringVariable) :

The above procedure is the reverse of the procedure Val. It is used to convert a Numeric Value into a String Variable.

NumericValue   It may be a numeric constant, numeric variable. It can be either real or integer.

StringVariable   A string Variable.

(e.g.)

```
Program Example (Input, Output);
Var
        St : string;
        Number : Integer;
Begin
        Number := 5688;
        Str(Number,St);
        Writeln(St);
        Writeln(St;
End.
```

Output

5688

The above program upon execution will give '5688' as its result.

RECURSION

So far we have seen some of the uses of procedures and functions. We have to bear in mind that in all the procedures and functions we have never tried to invoke the same procedure or function, with which we are working. Turbo Pascal also provides us a chance of calling the procedure and function by itself and this is called Recursion. When the procedure or function is properly called by itself, it reduces Program coding and in some cases it increases the efficiency of the Program. Thus, a recursion is a valuable tool for Programming. In this section, we shall see some of the pros and cons of recursion, when should we use, and not use recursion.

Now consider the following program code.

```
Function Fact (X : Integer) : Integer;
Begin
        If (X=1) then

            Fact := 1
        Else
            Fact := X * Fact(X-1);
End;
```

Recursion process is also called as "Back Substitution". Now let us see how this process works.

For example let us consider N=5

Since the value of N is not equal to 1, the function call

M : = fact(5)

   fact(5) = 5 * fact(4)

Subsequently,

    4 * fact(3)

        3 * fact(2)

            2 * fact(1)

and when n=1, the function returns the value as 1, and, therefore the fact = 5 * 4 * 3 * 2 * 1

Here is a complete program to demonstrate the concept of recursion.

```
Program Example (Input, Output);
Var
        N, M : Integer;
Function Fact( X : Integer ) : Integer;
Begin
        If (X=1) then
                Fact := 1
        Else
                Fact := X * Fact(X-1);
End;

{ Main Starts }
Begin
        Writeln('Enter Number to Find Factorial ');
        Readln(N)
        M := Fact(N);
        Writeln('The Factorial " ', M);
End.
```

Output

Enter Number to Find Factorial
5
The Factorial : 120

Wherever result is expressed in terms of successful application of the same solution to subsets of the problem, Recursion is found to work very successfully.

The important point to remember while developing a program (which uses the recursive feature is) the program should have an end condition which is usually done by using If statement. Failure to include the end condition will bring the system into crash.

The advantage of using recursion is, to reduce the program coding which will automatically make our program very clear to understand. Ofcourse most of the programs which employ the recursive feature can also be carried out by using the iterative concept, but, there are some programs which really expected to include this feature to make the programs so powerful and to provide elegance to the programs.

Exercises

1. Write a Procedure that interchanges the values of two variables.

2. a) Write a procedure in Pascal that will compute the trace of a matrix. The trace is defined as the sum of the diagonal elements of a matrix.

   b) Write a Pascal procedure to read N X N matrix and print the transpose of it.

3. A is a linear array containing at most N elements, Write a procedure which

   i) finds the largest value among the first K elements

   ii) Computes the sum of the first N elements.

   Write a Pascal program which uses the above procedure.

4. Write a program to return the minimum value in an array of reals using Procedure.

5. Construct a Pascal procedure to accept a number of unordered names from the keyboard and print the same in an alphabetical order on the display unit.

6. Using procedure, write a Pascal program that reads a sequence of characters into an array and counts the number of words that text contains. A word is any sequence of non-blank characters bounded on either side by at least one blank.

7. Write a procedure to encrept a sentence using the strategy of replacing a letter by the previous letter in its collating sequence, i.e. every A will be replaced by Z, every B by A and so on. Blanks are left undisturbed.

8. Write a Pascal program to count the number of characters and print the number of occurences of each vowel present in a given text.

9. What are formal parameters ? What is the parameter passing convention followed in Pascal.

10. Using procedure, write a program in Pascal to input a sequence of integers into an array and print five numbers per line.

11. What are global and local variables ? Discuss the scope of these variables ?.

12. Write a function which returns the area of a triangle.

13. What is a function ? Give the syntax of function subprogram.

14. Write a function to find the factorial of a given number and to find the value of

    NCR = N!/(N!(N–R)!).

15. Write a Program to find the sum of series of

    $Sin(x) = x - x^3/3! + x^5/5! -$ upto n terms.

16. Explain the function of Chr and Ord clearly specifying the type of parameters they accept and the type of value they return.

17. Write short notes on

    1. Value Parameter   2. Variable Parameter

18. Write a Pascal program to check the given square matrix of order N X N is singular or not.

19. Write similarities and dissimilarities between procedure and functions.

20. Whit is a recursion? Explain its execution process.

21. Write function subprogram to print the terms of the Fibonacci series 1,1,2,3,5,8.

22. What is the value of X printed by the following program?

```
Program Example (Input, Output);
Var
        X : Integer;
Procedure Find (X : Real);
     begin
            X := sqrt(X);
     end;
{main starts}
     begin
           X := 3;
           Find(X);
           Writeln(X);
     end.
```

a) 3 b) 1.7320080757 c) Run-time error d) none of the above

23. Consider the following Pascal function where A and B are nonzero positive integers. What is the value of Get (3,2)?

```
Function Get(A,B : Integer); Integer
begin
          if B := 0 then
             Get := 1
          else
             Get := 0
          else
          Get := Get(A-1,B)+Get(A-1,B-1)
end;
```

24. Following is a Pascal procedure for computing the transpose of an N X N (N > 1) matrix A of integers has an error. Find the error and correct it.

Assume that the following declarations are made in the main program.

```
Const
     Maxsize = 20;
type
     Intarr = Array [1..Maxsize, 1..Maxsize] of Integer;
Procedure Transpose (Var A : Intarr ; N : Integer);
Var
     I,J, Tmp : Integer;
begin
     for I := 1 to N-1 do
          for J := 1 to N do
               begin
                   Tmp := A[I,J];
                   A[J,I] := Tmp;
               end;
end;
```

25. Determine the number of divisors of 600.

26. Write a program using subprogram to exchange two values.

27. Write a program using recursion to find the factorial of N.

28. Write a program to convert Octal to decimal number using procedure.

29. Given two one-dimensional arrays A and B which sorted in ascending order. Write a program to merge them into a single sorted array C.

30. Write a program which will read a string and rewrite it in the alphabetical order. For example, the word **STRING** should be written as **GINRST**.

31. Write a recursive function subprogram to compute Schermann function for m=n=3.

    a (m,n) = n+1, if m=0
             = a(m−1) if n=0
             = a(m−1),a(m,n−1), otherwise

32. Write a subprogram to find the digits of a given number and use the subprogram to write a program to find if the given number contains any duplicate digits.

33. How the function and procedure differ, when called in the main program?

34. What is the type matching rule for a parameter of a procedure?

35. Explain the method of using global variable to pass a value to a procedure.

SOLVED PROBLEMS

1. Write a program to delete all vowels from a sentence. Assume that the sentence is nor more than 80 characters long.

```
Program Example ( Input,Output);
Type
          StrType = String ;
Var
          InStr,OutStr : StrType;
Procedure DeleteVowel ( Str1 : StrType;
                    Var Str2 : StrType );
Var
          I : Integer ;
          X : Char;
Begin
          Str2 :='';
          For I := 1 to Length(Str1) do
            Begin
              X := Upcase(Str1[i]);
              If (X <> 'A') And (X <> 'E') And (X <> 'I')
                  And (X <> 'O') And (X <> 'U') Then
                Str2 :=  Str2 + Str1[i];
            End;
End;

{ Main Starts }
Begin
       Writeln('Enter String ');
       Readln(InStr);
       DeleteVowel(InStr,OutStr);
       Writeln;
       Writeln('The String After Removing Vowels is ...');
       Writeln;
       Writeln(OutStr);
End.
```
Output

Enter String
Colour meets colour as if challenging each other
The String After Removing Vowels is ...
Clr mts clr s f chllngng ch thr

2. Write a Program to find the product of matrices of order 3 X 3 using Procedure

```
Program Example (Input,Output);
Type
        W = Array[1..3,1..3] of Integer ;
Var
        A,B,C : W;
Procedure MatGet(Var X : W);
Var
        I,J : Integer ;
Begin
        For I := 1 to 3 do
          For J := 1 to 3 do
             Readln(X[i,j]);
End;
Procedure MatMult( X,Y : W ;
                   Var Z : W );
Var
        I,J,K : Integer ;
Begin
        For I := 1 to 3 do
          For J := 1 to 3 do
               Begin
                  Z[i,j] := 0 ;
                    For K := 1 to 3 do
                       Z[i,j] := Z[i,j ]+ X[i,k] * Y[k,j] ;
               End;
End;
Procedure MatPrint( X : W );
Var
        I,J : Integer ;
Begin
        Writeln( 'The Output Matrix is ... ');
        For I := 1 to 3 do
           Begin
             For J := 1 to 3 do
                Write(X[i,j]:5);
             Writeln;
           End;
End;

{ Main Starts }
```

```
Begin
  Writeln('Enter 9 Elements for Array A ');
  MatGet(A);
  Writeln('Enter 9 Elements for Array B ');
  MatGet(B);
  MatMult(A,B,C);
  MatPrint(C);
End.
```

Output

Enter 9 Elements for Array A
1
2
3
4
5
6
7
8
9
Enter 9 Elements for Array B
1
2
3
4
5
6
7
8
9
The Output Matrix Is
30   36   42
66   81   96
102 126 150

3.   Write a Recursive function to sum integer numbers between 1-100.

```
Program Example (Input,Output);
Var
         Sum : Integer ;
Function Sum1to100 (N : integer ) : Integer ;
```

```
Begin
        If (n=1) then
            Sum1to100 := n
        Else
            Sum1to100 := n+sum1to100(n-1);
End;
{Main Starts}
Begin
        Sum:=Sum1to100(100);
        Writeln('Sum 1 to 100 is ',Sum);
End.
```

Output

Sum 1 to 100 is 5050

4.   Write a program to search whether the given number is present or not by using function.

```
Program Example (Input, Output);
Type
        W = Array[1..5] of Integer;
Var
        A : W;
        I,X : Integer;
Function Lsearch (Var N : W; M : Integer) : Boolean;
Var
        J : Integer
        B : Boolean;
Begin
        J := 1; B := true;
        While ( (J<=5) and (B) ) do
            Begin
            If ( n[J] = X ) then
              B:=False;
              J:=J+1;
            End;
        If (B) then
            Lsearch:=False
        else
            Lsearch:=True;
End;
```

```
{Main Starts}
Begin
        Writeln('Enter 5 Numbers 1 by 1');
        For I:=1 to 5 do
            Readln(a[I];
        Writeln('Enter Search No');
        Readln(X);
        If (Lsearch(A,X) Then
            Writeln('The Given Number Is There');
        else
            Writeln('The Given Number Is Not There');
End.
```

Output

Enter 5 Numbers 1 by 1
34
56
12
887
233
Enter Search No
12
The Given Number Is There

Enter 5 Numbers 1 by 1
123
453
674
987
342
Enter Search No
888

The Given Number is Not There

5. Write a function to find whether given value is available in an array of size 100 integers arranged in the ascending order using binary search method print the position of the value in the array if the value is found, otherwise print 0.

```
Program Example (Input,Output);
Type
        W = Array[1..100] of Integer ;
Var
        A     : W ;
        I,N,ASize : Integer ;
Function SearchNo ( X : W ;
            No,ArrySize : Integer ) :Integer ;
Var
        High,Low,Mid : Integer ;

{Procedure Selection Sort Begins }

Procedure SelectionSort Var Y : W ;
            NoOfElmnts : Integer );
Var
        I,J,Small : Integer ;

        { Procedure For Swap }

        Procedure Swap ( Var P,Q : Integer );
        Var
          T : Integer ;
        Begin
          T := P ; P := Q ; Q := T ;
        End;
Begin
        For I := 1 to NoOfElmnts-1 do
        Begin
          Small := I ;
          For J := 1+1 to NoOfElmnts do
            If (Y[J] < Y[Small] ) then
                    Small := J ;
          Swap ( Y[I],Y[Small]);
        End;
End;

{ Function Main For Search }
Begin
        SelectionSort(X,ArrySize);
        Low := 0;
        High := ArrySize;
        High := High = 1 ;
```

```
          While (High < > Low + 1) do
              Begin
                 Mid := (Low + High) Div 2;
                 If (X[Mid] <= No) then
                    Low := Mid
                 else
                    High := Mid;
              End;
          If (X[Low] = No) then
              SearchNo := 1
          else
              SearchNo := 0;
End;

{Main Starts}

Begin
   Writeln('How Many Nos Are You Going to Enter');
   Readln(Asize);
   Writeln('Enter', Asize, 'Elements 1 by 1');
   For I := 1 to Asize do
   Readln (A[I]);
   Writeln('Enter Search No');
   Readln(N);
   If (SearchNo(A,N,Asize)=1) then
     Writeln('Given Number is Present in the Array')
   Else
     Writeln('Given Number is Not Present in the Array');
End.
```

Output

How Many Nos Are you Going to Enter
5
Enter 5 Elements 1 by 1
78
54
987
764
566

Enter Search No
987

Given Number is Present in the Array

How Many Nos Are you Going to Enter
4

Enter 4 Elements 1 by 1
87
34
342
12

Enter Search No
100
Given Number is Not Present in the Array

Chapter - 7

RECORDS

So far we have seen simple data types, such as int, real, char and boolean. In this chapter, we switch our concentration to a special data type called Record which will open our way to enter into modern programming concepts. It follows Array in structured data type category.

A Record is a collection of variables. The variables in a Record can be of different types such as Char, Int, Real or Boolean. It deviates from array in this aspect wherein all the variables must be of the same data type. Elements in a record are called the members of the structure. We will discuss the features of a record in the forthcoming sections.

Record Declaration

Record can be declared in two ways either through type declaration or through variable declaration. Let us see how a record can be declared through type declaration.

```
Record_Name = Record
              --------------------------- ;
              Members and their data type ;
              --------------------------- ;
          End ;
```

We begin with a record that contains three variables — a string, an integer and a real. This record represents a student record in a class. The structure is as follows.

```
Stdrec = Record
        Name : string ;
        Examno : Integer ; .
        Ave : Real ;
        End ;
```

The keyword record introduces the specifier. Here the record name is **Stdrec.** As it is merely a declaration, it does not occupy any space in the memory. It is to show how a record variable will look when it is defined.

Defining a Record Variable

Before assigning any value to the members of the record, it should be defined as a record variable. Consider the following construct

```
Var
        Markrec : Stdrec ;
```

This defines Markrec as a variable of type Stdrec. This definition causes to reserve sufficient space in memory for Markrec.

Accessing Member of a Record

Once a record variable has been defined, its members can be accessed using a period (.), also called the dot or member operator. The following illustration will show how a value is assigned to the members in a record.

```
        Markrec. Name := 'Thiagarajar' ;
        Markrec.No := 1234;
        Markrec.Ave := 89.67;
```

From the above it can be seen that the member in a record can be accessed through its record name. The syntax for accessing an element in a record is as follows.

```
        RecordName.MemberName;
```

Here is a simple program to illustrate how a record can be used in a program.

```
Program Example (Input, Output);
Type
      Stdrec = Record
                    Name : String;
                    Tam, Eng, Mat : Integer ;
               End;
Var
        Markrec : Stdrec ;
        Tot : Integer ;
        Ave : Real;
Begin
  Writeln ('Enter Student Name ');
  Readln (Markrec.Name) ;
  Writeln ('Enter Marks for Tamil, English , Maths ');
  Readln (Markrec.Tam,Markrec.Eng , Markrec.Mat) ;
  Tot := Markrec.Tam + Markrec.Eng + Markrec.Mat;
  Ave := Tot / 3 ;
  Writeln ('Student Name : ' Markrec.Name) ;
  Writeln ('Total Marks : ',Tot) ;
  Writeln ('Average : ',Ave:5:2) ;
End.
```

Output

Enter Student Name
Sivakumar
Enter Marks for Tamil , English , Maths
76 81 89
Student Name: Sivakumar
Total Marks : 246
Average : 82.00

Another method for declaring a record variable is through variable declaration.

The declaration is as follows.

```
Var
Markrec : Record
              Name : String;
              Tam,Eng,Mat : Integer ;
          End;
Tot     : Integer ;
Ave     : Real;
```

The above method declares record variable directly. This method of declaration may be used as an advantage, when there is no need to pass a Record to a Procedure or Function.

With Structure

In previous program we have used a record consists of 4 fields and it is possible to refer the variables through the dot operator. However we may have situations wherein we have more number of fields in a Record. To overcome this shortcoming Turbo Pascal provides us the **with** structure. The usage of this structure is as follows.

With RecordVariable Do

> **Begin**
>
> —— ;
>
> **End;**

Now, let us record the nutshell of the first program using the with structure.

```
With Markrec do
```

```
Begin
  Writeln('Enter Student Name ');
  Readln(Name);
  Writeln('Enter Marks for Tamil , English , Maths ');
  Readln(Tam,Eng,Mat);
  Tot :=Tam + Eng + Mat;
  Ave := Tot / 3 ;
End;
```

In the above program , inside the with structure the statement

Readln (Name) is equivalent to **Readln (Markrec.Name)**; and

Readln (Tam, Eng, Mat) is equivalent to

Readln (Markrec.Tam, Markrec.Eng, Markrec.Mat);

We will now write a complete program by incorporating all the things that we have seen so far.

```
Program Example (Input,Output);
Type
        Stdrec = Record
                    Name : String;
                    Tam,Eng,Mat : Integer ;
                 End;
Var
        Markrec : Stdrec ;
        Tot : Integer ;
        Ave : Real;
Begin
   With Markrec do
   Begin
      Writeln('Enter Student Name ');
      Readln(Name);
      Writeln('Enter Marks for Tamil , English , Maths ');
      Readln (Tam,Eng,Mat);
      Tot := Tam + Eng + Mat;
      Ave := Tot / 3 ;
   End;
```

```
        Writeln ('Student Name : ',Markrec.Name);
        Writeln ('Total Marks : ',Tot);
        Writeln ('Average : ',Ave:5:2) ;
End.
```

Output

Enter Student Name
Premkumar
Enter Marks for Tamil , English , Maths
78 87 69
Student Name : Premkumar
Total Marks : 234
Average : 78.00

Array of Records

Similar to the case where we have array of integers or reals, we also
have array of records. It finds useful application in record manipulations
such as to compare records, to arrange records in a particular sequence
etc.,. The declaration of array of records is similar to that of declaration
of simple data type.

The declaration is

```
Var
     Markrec : Array [1..5] of Stdrec ;
```

This creates 5 sets of record that are organised as defined in the record
Stdrec, where stdrec is already declared through a type declaration
statement ;

```
        Stdrec = Record

                Name : String;
                Tam,Eng,Mat : Integer ;
        End;
```

Accessing of a member from such an array of records also follows the
same rules as in the case of simple data type array declarations.

For example, to access the fields Name,Tam,Eng and Mat of the first
record, the following code is used :

```
  Readln (Stdrec[i].Name);
  Readln (Stdrec [i].Tam,Stdrec[i].Eng,Stdrec[i].Mat);
```

The program coding for receiving the details of the marks of the 5 students, using the above statement in a with structure, embedded within a for loop is as follows

The program is also designed to find the total marks and the average marks for the given 5 students.

```
Program Example (Input,Output);
Type
          Stdrec = Record
                          Name :String;
                          Tam,Eng,Mat : Integer ;
                    End;
Var
          Markrec : Array[1..5] of Stdrec ;
          Tot : Array[1..5] of Integer ;
          Ave : Array[1..5]of Real;
          I : Integer ;
Begin
   For I:= 1 to 5 do
     With Markrec [i] do
       Begin
         Writeln('Enter Student Name -> ');
         Readln(Name);
         Writeln('Enter Marks for Tamil , English , Maths ->');
         Readln (Tam,Eng,Mat);
         Tot[i] := Tam + Eng + Mat;
         Ave[i] := Tot[i] / 3 ;
       End;
         Writeln;
         Writeln('   Student Name      Total     Average');
         Writeln;
         For I:= 1 to 5 do
         Writeln(Markrec[i].Name:15,'',Tot[i]:5,'',Ave[i]):5:2);
End.
```

Output

Enter Student Name ---> Ramesh
Enter Marks for Tamil , English , Maths ---> 89 68 79
Enter Student Name ---> Rajan
Enter Marks for Tamil , English , Maths ---> 62 75 78
Enter Student Name ---> Kishore
Enter Marks for Tamil , English , Maths ---> 71 93 91
Enter Student Name ---> Sivakumar

Enter Marks for Tamil , English , Maths ——> 67 98 91
Enter Student Name ——> Ramalingam
Enter Marks for Tamil , English , Maths ——> 67 62 71

Student Name	Total	Average
Ramesh	236	78.67
Rajan	215	71.67
Kishore	255	85.00
Sivakumar	256	85.33
Ramalingam	200	66.67

Let us further dig into array of records by another example. The following program is an example to arrange a set of records in a particular fashion. The record consists of the following details.

EmpName	Employee Name
Bp	Basic Pay
Da	Dearness Allowance
Allo	Other Allowances
Dedn	Deductions

The Program uses Totpay as a Key field and it is calculated as

Totpay = BP + Da + Allo — Dedn

```
Program Example (Input,Output) ;
Type
        Salrec = Record

                  EmpName : String ;
                  Bp,Da,Allo,Dedn : Integer ;
                End ;
Var
    Emprec        : Array [1..5] of Salrec ;
    Totpay        : Array [1..5] of Integer ;
    I,J,Temppay   : Integer ;
    Temprec       : Salrec;
Begin
        For I := 1 to 5 do
            With Emprec [I] do
```

```
            Begin
                Write('Enter Employee Name : ') ;
                Readln (EmpName) ;
                Write ('Enter Bp,Da,Allo,Dehn : ');
                Readln (Bp,Da,Allo,Dedn);
                Totpay[I] := Bp + Da + Allo - Dedn ;

            End;

{Sorting Begins}

            For I:= 1 to 4 do
                For J:= i+1 to 5 do
                    If (Totpay[I] ,Totpay[J]) then
                        Begin
                            Temprec  : Emprec [I];
                            Emprec[I] := Emprec[J];
                            Emprec[J] := Temprec;
                            Temppay := Totpay[I];
                            Totpay[I] := Totpay[J] ;
                            Totpay[J] := Temppay;
                        End;
Writeln;
Writeln (' Sored output as Follows ') ;
Writeln;
Writeln('  Name Totpay') ;
Writeln;
   For I := 1 to 5 do
   Writeln (Emprec[I] .EmpName:15,' ',Totpay[I] :5) ;
End.
```

Output

Enter Employee Name : Karthikeyan
Enter Bp,Da,Allo,Dedn : 1250 240 125 250
Enter Employee Name : Kathirvelan
Enter Bp,Da,Allo,Dedn : 2050 300 100 325
Enter Employee Name : Kannan
Enter Bp,Da,Allo,Dedn : 1750 400 125 350
Enter Employee Name : Kalaichelvan
Enter Bp,Da,Allo,Dedn : 2100 300 150 180
Enter Employee Name : Saravanan
Enter Bp,Da,Allo,Dedn : 1800 250 100 230

Sorted Output as Follows

Name	Totpay
Kalaichelvan	2370
Kathirvelan	2125
Kannan	1925
Saravanan	1920
Karthikeyan	1365

Explanation

When tracing the above program one can notice that record variables can also be assigned in a manner similar to simple data type variable assignment. The program segment

```
Temprec := Emprec[i];
```

implies that the content of ith record of **Emprec** is totally assigned to **Temprec** which is already declared as the same record type as **Emprec**.

Arrays within Record

We have already seen that simple data types can be used inside a record. The use of arrays as record elements is also permitted and we can use one, two or multidimensional arrays, of any data type (integer, real, character or boolean) inside the record.

Consider the following record declaration

```
Type
      Stdrec = Record
                  Name : String ;
                  Subs : Array [1..2] of integer ;
               End;
      Var
         Markrec : Array [1..2] of stdrec ;
```

Here, the member subs contain two elements subs (1) and subs (2), representing the marks obtained in two the subjects.

The statement ,

```
Markrec[2].Sub[2]
```

refers to the 2nd markrecord and the marks obtained in 2nd subject. The program following will explain how arrays are used within a record.

```
Program Example (Input,Output);
Type
        Stdrec = Record
                    Name : String;
                    Subs : Array[1..2] of integer ;
                 End;
Var
    Markrec : Array[1..2] of Stdrec ;
    Tot : Array[1..2] of Integer ;
    I,J : Integer ;
Begin
        For I:= 1 to 2 do
          With Markrec [i] do
              Begin
                 Writeln('Enter Name : ');
                 Readln(Name);
                 Tot[i]:= O;
                 Writeln('Enter 2 Marks ');
                    For J := 1 to 2 do
                       Begin
                             Readln(Subs[j]);
                             Tot[i] := Tot[i] + Subs[j];
                       End;
              End;
Writeln;
Writeln('   Name     Sub-1    Sub-2    Total ');
For I:= 1 to 2 do
        With Markrec [i] do
            Begin
               Write(Name:15);
                  For j := 1 to 2 do
                     Write(Subs[j]:12);
               Writeln(Tot[i]:12);
            End;
End.
```

Output

Enter Name
Prakash
Enter 2 Marks
67
74
Enter Name
Soundar
Enter 2 Marks
83
82

Name	Sub-1	Sub-2	Total
Prakash	67	74	141
Soundar	83	82	165

Passing a Record to a Procedure.

In Turbo Pascal, passing a record to a procedure is similar as passing an array to a procedure. When we are passing an array to a procedure, it is declared through a type declaration statement in the procedure. In a similar way, records are also declared through Type declaration statements in the procedure.

Let us examine the following program to get a good idea, on passing a record to a procedure, still further.

```
Program Example (Input,Output);
Type
        Book = Record
                  Title : String ;
                  Author : String ;
                  Price : Real ;
               End;
Var
     Bookrec : Book ;
Procedure GetBookDetail( Var TBook : Book );
Begin
     With TBook Do
       begin
           Writeln('Enter Book Name ');
           Readln(Title);
           Writeln('Author Name ');
```

```
            Readln(Author);
            Writeln('Price');
            Readln(Price);
        End;
End;

Procedure PutBookDetail( TBook : Book );
Begin
        With TBook Do
          Begin
                Writeln('Book Name : ',Title);
                Writeln('Author Name : ',Author);
                Writeln(' Price : ',Price:5:2);
          End;
End;

{ Main Starts }
Begin
        GetBookDetail(Bookrec);
        Writeln;
        PutBookDetail(Bookrec);
End.
```

Output

Enter Book Name
Basic Programming
Author Name
E. Balagurusamy
Price
63.00

Book Name : Basic Programming
Author Name : E. Balagurusamy
Price : 63.00

The procedure **GetBookDetail** is used to receive details of the book from the user. Please note that in the declaration of the record variable, Book is declared as a variable parameter. Hence , it can pass whatever be the information received by this procedure , to the main program for future reference.

The procedure **PutDetailBook** is used to display, information regarding the book in a neat format. Here, the record variable Book, is declared as a value parameter as there is no need to pass anything to the main program.

Nested Records

A record can also act as an element in another record and such structures are called Nested records. Consider the following declaration

```
Dob = Record
        Date : Integer ;
        Month : String ;
        Year : Integer ;
      End;
```

Dob (Data of Birth) is a record type which contains date, month and year as elements. It is substituted in another record named StdInfo, as Bday(Birthday) and a complete declaration is as follows.

```
StdInfo = Record
            Name: String;
            Age : Integer ;
            Bday: Dob;
          End;
```

Before using StdInfo in our program, it is declared as a record variable as usual in the variable section.

```
Var
        StdInfoRec : Stdinfo ;
```

Now the record variable StdInfoRec will have name, age, date, month and year as its members.

The members **Name** and **Age** of the **StdInfoRec**, are accessed by using normal dot operator. The fields in **Bday** such as **date, month** and **year** are accessed by linking all the record variable (from outer record to the inner record) using the dot operator.

The program which uses the above structure is as follows.

```
Program Example (Input, Output) ;
Type
        Dob = Record
                Date : Integer ;
                Month : String;
                Year : Integer ;
              End;
```

```
                        StdInfo = Record
                                    Name : String;
                                    Age  : Integer ;
                                    Bday : Dob;
                                 End;
Var
        StdInfoRec : StdInfo ;

Begin
     With StdInfoRec do
        Begin
          Writeln ('Enter Name ');
          Readln (Name);
          Writeln ('Age');
          Readln (Age) ;
            With Bday do
              Begin
                Writeln ('Enter Date ');
                Readln (Date) ;
                Writeln ('Month');
                Readln (Month) ;
                Writeln ('Year');
                Readln (Year) ;
              End;
        End;
Writeln;
Writeln ('The Given Information .. ');
          Writeln ('Name  : ' , StdInfoRec.Name) ;
          Writeln ('Age   : ' , StdInfoRec.Age) ;
          Writeln ('Date  : ' , StdInfoRec.Date) ;
          Writeln ('Month : ' , StdInfoRec.Month) ;
          Writeln ('Year  : ' , StdInfoRec.Year) ;
End.
```

Output

Enter Name
Ramesh
Age
23
Enter Date
24
Month

Sept
Year
1971
The Given Information ....

Name   :   Ramesh

Age :   23

Date :   24

Month   :   Sept

Year :   1971

Variant Records

It is one of the special features which make Pascal very powerful among the computer language. Though the name sounds strange to BASIC or FORTRAN programmers, it is a powerful programming tool. It has the property to vary its fields depending on the type of the data to be stored and hence the name. The general format is as follows.

```
Record-Name = Record
                Declaration ;
                Case tag-identifier = Data type of
                Case label_1 : (field declaration) ;
                Case label_2 : (field declaration) ;
              End;
```

Depending upon the tag-identifier, field declaration will be taken into account.

Now let us see how it is realised through an example program.

The program is designed to receive an option first. If the option is equal to 1, the user has to enter 2 subjects and if the option is equal to 2, then the user has to feed 3 subjects.

```
Program Example (Input, Output) ;
Var
   Stdrec : Record
               Name : String ;
               Case Option : Integer of
                  1 : ( Tamil,English : Integer ) ;
                  2 : ( Hindi,Malayalam,Telugu:Integer);
           End;
```

```
                    Tot : Integer ;
Begin
       With Stdrec do
          Begin
              Writeln( 'Enter Name ');
              Readln(Name);
              Writeln('Type 1 For 2 Papers and 2 For 3 Papers ');
              Readln(Option);

             If (Option=1) Then
                Begin
                  Writeln('Enter Marks For Tamil,English ');
                  Readln(Tamil, English);
                  Tot := Tamil + English ;
                End
             Else
                  Begin
                    Writeln('Enter Marks For Hindi,Telugu & Malayalam ');
                    Readln(Hindi,Telugu,Malayalam);
                    Tot := Hindi + Telugu + Malayalam ;
                  End;
          End;

       Writeln;
       Writeln( 'Name : ',Stdrec.Name);
       Writeln(' Total : ',Tot);
End.
```

Output

Enter Name
Raja
Type 1 For 2 Papers and 2 For 3 Papers
1
Enter Marks For Tamil,English
62 78

Name : Raja
Total : 140

Enter Name
Jothi
Type 1 For 2 Papers and 2 For 3 Papers

2
Enter Marks For Hindi,Telugu & Malayalam
56 77 91
Name : Jothi
Total : 224

Now we know how to use variant records when it has simple data types. The following program will illustrate how a structured data type such as an array is used in the variant records. When the user's choice is 1 the elements for the array **Mpc** is received from the programmer. If the choice is 2 then the elements for the array **Ceah** is received from the user. Here is a program to fulfil the above idea.

```
Program Example (Input,Output);
Var
          Stdrec : Record
                  Name : String ;
                  Case Choice : Integer of
                  1 : ( Mpc : Array[1..3] of Integer );
                  2 : ( Ceah : Array[1..4] of Integer );
                  End;
          Tot,I : Integer ;
Begin
  With Stdrec do
   Begin
    Writeln( 'Enter Name ');
    Readln(Name);
    Writeln('Type 1 For 3 Subjects and 2 For 4 Subjects ');
    Readln(Choice);
    Tot :=0;

    If (Choice=1) Then
     Begin
     Writeln('Enter Marks for Maths,Physics,Chemistry 1 by 1 ');
          For i := 1 to 3 do
          Begin
                Readln(Mpc[i]);
                Tot := Tot + Mpc [i] ;
          End;
     End
     Else
      Begin
       Writeln('Enter Marks For Com, Eco, Acc, His. 1 by 1');
```

```
                    For i := 1 to 4 do
                        Begin
                            Readln (Ceah [i]) ;
                            Tot := Tot + Ceah [i] ;
                        End;
        End;
    End;
            Writeln;
            Writeln ( 'Name' : ',Stdrec.Name) ;
            Writeln ( 'Total : ',Tot) :
End.
```

Output

Enter Name
Anbu
Type 1 for 3 Subjects and 2 For 4 Subjects
1
Enter Marks For Maths, Physics, Chemistry 1 by 1
67
72
91
Name : Anbu
Total : 230

Enter Name
Rajkumar
Type 1 For 3 Subjects and 2 For 4 Subjects
2
Enter Marks For Com, Eco, Acc, His 1 by 1
71
82
78
91
Name : Rajkumar
Total : 322

Now we can understand the concept of records and are familiar with the
With structure, Array of records, Arrays within record, Passing a record
to a procedure, Nested records and Variant records through some
example programs.

Exercises

1. What is meant by Record. Write the rules for defining a record type.

2. What is the purpose of With structure. Summarise the rules for using With structure.

3. Define a Record structure for storing a complete home address.

4. Declare a structure with following fields

   Employee number - an integer quantity

   Employee name - a string of characters

   Age - integer

   Designation - string of characters

   Write Pascal statements to assign values to the various fields and print them out with appropriate messages.

5. What is a variant record structure. What are the rules to be followed while creating such structure.

6. Write a Pascal program to read a set of names and print them in the alphabetical order using records within records.

7. Describe how variable size records are defined in Pascal. Explain any 2 situations where variable size records are needed.

8. Write a program in Pascal using records to read a set of students names and their marks in a neat tabular format.

9. Using the scope rules of Pascal determine the declarations that apply to each occurrence of the names A and B in the following program segment.

```
Procedure T ( U,V,X,Y : Integer ) ;
Var
          A : Record
                A,B : Integer :
              end ;
          B : Record
                B,A : Integer;
              end;
```

```
Begin
              With A do
                   begin
                       A := 4;
                       B := V;
                   end;
              With B do
                   begin
                       A := X;
                       B := Y;
                   end ;
End.
```

10. A variant record in Pascal is defined by

```
type
              Varirec = Record
                          Number : Integer ;
                            Case ( Var1 , Var2 ) of
                                var1 : (x,y : Integer ) ;
                                Var2 : (p,Q : Real ) ;
                            end;
                        end;
```

Suppose an array of 100 such records was declared on a machine which uses 4 bytes for an integer and 8 bytes for a real. How much space would the compiler have to reserve for the array ?

a) 2800 b) 2400 c) 2000 d) 1200

11. Write a program to create 10 records with the following members :

(i) Name   (ii) RegNo   (iii) Mark

(iv) Degree   (v) Major

also find the maximum marks among these to records and display that record on the screen.

12. Write a program using records that converts Cartesian co-ordinates to polar co-ordinates and vice versa.

13. What is the total memory in bytes required to store S1.

```
Type
  Studrec = record
               name :  array[1..20] of char;
               id : integer
               case financeaid of
                  true : amount : real;
                         total : real,
                  false : pastaid : boolean;
            end;
     Var S1 : Studrec
```

CHAPTER - 8

FILES

The study of any language will be completed only after knowing about the file handling capability of the language. If we want to process small volume of data then the methods we have seen so far will be enough. A significant drawback of the earlier methods is that once the program is over the data may no longer be alive. But we may want to store the information for a quite long time. So, to overcome this difficulty and as well as to process huge volume of records we require files.

In this chapter we shall see how files are used to facilitate our requirement, through numerous examples.

Organisation of files

File organisation falls into two categories in Turbo Pascal. They are

    i. Sequential Organisation

    ii. Random Organisation

In sequential organisation, the records have to be entered in a proper sequence. During processing, the records get processed in the same sequence as they were entered. Let us assume that we are having 10 records and we have entered them one by one. During the processing of these records, the first record entered will be rolled out first, then the second record and so on. This method is called **First in First out (Fifo).** In this organisation it is not possible to process intermediate records without disturbing the neighbouring records. This type of processing will be much used where all the records need to be processed. A typical example for such an organisation is the Cassette Recorder in which we hear prerecorded songs one after the other.

In random organisation we can enter records in any arbitrary manner. During processing it is quire possible to process the intermediate records without disturbing the other records. This method of organisation is found to be very useful where processing of records require an arbitrary manner. A typical example for such an organisation is the Record Player where we can directly access any of our desired song by simply moving the stylus. Hence, this method of organisation is also called Direct Access method.

Turbo Pascal provides basically two types of disk files

i)   Binary files
ii) Text files

The method of storing data in binary files follows the same format as that which is stored in computer's internal memory. It is not possible to read the contents of the data file as it contains non printable characters. It is further classified into typed and untyped file. In typed binary file, the data can be read from an existing file and written to another file regardless of its data type as it does not have any specific data type.

Turbo Pascal also supports a special type of file handling facility called Text file handling. This method is very useful in processing of text matters such as to print text message, to count or to replace a particular character or word, etc. The latter part of this chapter is devoted to deal with this, in greater detail with examples.

Typed Binary file

Now let us see how typed binary files can be used to enhance the file handling. To start with we have to declare a file variable. The declaration of typed binary file variable is exactly to other variable declarations.

The general form is as follows :

```
Var
   Var.Name : File of data-type ;
```
Here   ·

Variable name is the typed binary file's variable name. The data type which is defined already may be integer or real or even a record type.

Once the file variable id defined, the next step is the opening of the file. The file is opened by using a procedure called Assign and the general form is as follows:

```
Assign (file variable, file name);
```
here

file variable is also called as internal reference to the file which is declared previously in the declaration part.

file name is also called as external reference or directory reference to the file.

The rules to be followed while naming a file is that, a file name (also called primary name) should not contain more than eight characters. A file may or may not have an extension name (also called secondary name). If it has, it should not exceed three characters, which is used to identify the type of the file. Some of the valid file names are shown below:

TEMP.DAT STDREC.DAT SALES.FIL BUDGET94.TXT

It is not adviceable to give extension name such as .C, .FOR, .BAS, .COB , .PAS as they confuse with source code for that corresponding languages.

Note that in an Assign procedure we have given both the internal reference and the external reference for a file. Within the program whenever we want to refer the external reference it is enough that we refer the internal reference of the particular file.

Normally when a file is opened the basic operation we are going to do with the file is as follows:

i) Add information to a fresh file.

ii) Read information from an existing file.

iii) Append Information to an existing file.

To add information (records) to a fresh file, we are using another procedure named as Rewrite and the general form for Rewrite is given below

```
Rewrite(file variable);
```

It is the variable for the file to be opened.

The above procedure should be used very carefully, because if this procedure is used with an already existing file, the Rewrite procedure will flush out the contents of the existing file and make the file a fresh one.

To read information (records) from an existing file, the procedure Reset will be used. The syntax is as follows.

```
Reset (file variable) ;
```

It is the variable for the file to be opened.

If this procedure is used without having an external reference in the Assign procedure, Reset will issue an error message during run time.

To add information to an existing file we may use the append procedure. This procedure is only applicable to text file and will be seen in the later part of this book.

Now we will see how a record (data items) can be written to a file. For this, we have another procedure in the name of Write and the syntax is as follows:

```
Write (file variable,Record name);
```

Here, file variable is a variable to which the file can write the data. Here data items can also be written individually, separating them by commas or we can directly write all the data items through its record name.

Similar to that of Write procedure for writing data items to a file, we have a procedure called Read, which is used to read a record (data items) from an existing file. The general form for this procedure is as follows:

```
Read (file variable, Record name);
```

Where file variable is a variable from which the file can read the data. Here, instead of reading data items one by one it is quite possible to read complete record directly just by giving its record name. This also gives clarity to the program.

All files opened for processing should be closed after completing necessary action. Failure to close a file will invite catastrophic effect. The general form to close a file is as follows:

```
Close (file variable) ;
```

where file variable is the variable for the file to be closed.

Now, let us develop a file which uses sequential file organisation. In file handling, we have to develop two programs. The first program is used to receive data items from the user and no calculations are performed in this program. The second program is used to process the entered data. All calculations are carried out only in the processing file.

Let us create a data entry program. The program is designed in such a way to receive data items from the use until the user desires to stop. This is carried out by using a variable **'Cont',** and it is initialised as **'Y'**.The **Do-while loop** is used for the job to receive the data items from the user until **'Cont'** retains the value **'Y'**.

The record contains the following items

Variable Name	Type
Name	String
Examno	Integer
Tamil	Integer
English	Integer
Maths	Integer

Here is a program which illustrates the use of keywords which we have studied so far.

```
Program Example (Input,Output) ;
Type
            Stdrec : Record
                        Name    : String ;
                        Examno  : Integer ;
                        Tamil   : Integer ;
                        English : Integer ;
                        Maths   : Integer ;
                     End;
Var
        Markrec : Stdrec ;
        Infile : File of Stdrec;
        Cont : Char;
Begin
        Assign (Infile,'Mark.Dat');
        Rewrite (Infile) ;
        Cont := 'Y' ;
        While (cont = 'Y') Do
          Begin
            With Markrec Do
              Begin
              Write ('Enter Name : ');
              Readln(Name) ;
              Write(' Examno : ');
              Readln(Examno) ;
              Write(' Tamil : ') ;
              Readln(Tamil) ;
              Write(' English : ');
```

```
                    Readln(English) ;
                    Write(' Maths : ');
                    Readln(Maths);
                    Write(Infile,Markrec);
                    End;
              Write('Want To Proceed (Y/N) ');
              Readln(Cont) ;
              End;
Close(Infile) ;
End.
```

Output

Enter Name : Manian
Examno : 1001
Tamil : 56
English : 78
Maths : 98
Want To Proceed (Y/N) Y
Enter Name : Suresh
Examno : 1002
Tamil : 44
English : 67
Maths : 78
Want to Proceed (Y/N) Y
Enter Name : Jayakumar
Examno : 1003
Tamil : 65
English : 87
Maths 91
Want To Proceed (Y/N) N

Now our job is to process the entered data in desired manner. The following program reads the content of the above entered file and computes the total and average mark for every student. The following program also employs a special boolean function Eof ( ); which returns either true or false while processing. It returns true after processing the contents of the given file variable, if not, it returns false till the record pointer reaches end of file. Here is a program which demonstrates the same.

```
Program Example (Input,Output)
Type
    Stdrec = Record
```

```
                    Name    :  String ;
                    Examno  :  Integer ;
                    Tamil   :  Integer ;
                    English :  Integer ;
                    Maths   :  Integer ;
                End;
Var
    Markrec: Stdrec ;
    Infile : File of Stdrec;
    Tot    : Integer ;
    Ave    : Real;
Begin
    Assign(Infile,'Mark.Dat');
    Reset(Infile);
    While Not Eof(Infile) Do
            Begin
              With Markrec Do
                Begin
                    Read(Infile,Markrec);
                    Tot:= Tamil + English + Maths ;
                    Ave := Tot/ 3;
                    Writeln('Name       : ', Name);
                    Writeln('Exam No  : ',Examno);
                    Writeln('Tamil      : ',Tamil);
                    Writeln('English  : ',English);
                    Writeln('Maths     : ',Maths);
                    Writeln('Total     : ',Tot);
                    Writeln('Average  : ',Ave:5:2);
                    Writeln;
                End;
                  Write('Press Any Key To Proceed ');
                  Readln;
                  Writeln;
            End;
Close(Infile);
End.
```

Output

```
Name      :  Manian
Exam No   :  1001
Tamil     :  56
English   :  78
```

Maths   :   98
Total   :   232
Average   :   77.33

Press Any Key To Proceed

Name   :   Suresh
Exam No   :   1002
Tamil   :   44
English   :   67
Maths   :   78
Total   :   189
Average   : 63.00

Press Any Key To Proceed

Name   :   Jayakumar
Exam No   :   1003
Tamil   :   65
English   :   87
Maths   :   91
Total   :   243
Average   :   81.00

Press Any Key To Proceed

From the above two illustrations we have seen how to create a binary file and also to process the same. Now we focus our attention on how to add a record to an existing binary file. It is nothing but a process of adding a record at the end of an existing file. Although the procedure **Append** is available, it is intended only for the handling of Text file. So, we have to write our own routine to perform the above mentioned processing.

In this process the file should be opened by using the standard procedure Assign followed by **Reset.** Then the following routine is used to move the record pointer to the end of the file.

```
While not eof(infile) do
Read(infile,Markrec);
```

After this, the usual procedure starts to add records to the end of the file as long as it is desired. Here is a complete program to demonstrate the above concept clearly.

```
Program Example (Input,Output);
Type
     Stdrec = Record
                    Name : String ;
                    Examno : Integer ;
                    Tamil : Integer ;
                    English : Integer ;
                    Maths : Integer ;
               End;
Var
     Markrec : Stdrec ;
     Infile : File of Stdrec;
     Cont : Char;
Begin
          Assign(Infile,'Mark.Dat');
          Reset(Infile);
          While Not eof(Infile) do
            Read(infile,Markrec);
          Cont := 'Y' ;
          While (Cont = 'Y') Do
            Begin
                  With Markrec Do
                    Begin
                          Write('Enter Name : ');
                          Readln(Name);
                          Write('  Examno : ');
                          Readln(Examno);
                          Write('  Tamil : ');
                          Readln(Tamil);
                          Write('  English : ');
                          Readln(English);
                          Write('  Maths  : ');
                          Readln(Maths);
                          Writeln(Infile,Markrec);
                    End;
                          Write('Want To Proceed (Y/N)');
                          Readln(Cont);
            End;
Close(Infile);
End.
```

To get the output for the above program run the processing file of the previous one.

TEXT FILE

It is one of the special features which is not found in other languages such as BASIC, FORTRAN. This one is mainly used to handle the manipulation of text. For example, if we wish to count the number of vowels in a file or to replace a particular character with another one, this text file may be used. In this case, the file variable is declared as Text as we are going to enter only text messages. The other keywords for opening a file, closing a file and mode setting are the same as the binary file. Here Writeln is used to write the messages to a file though Write is also permitted. The difference is, messages in a file is continuous if we use Write, and it is line by line if we use Writeln. Ofcourse, it is our choice to choose according to our needs. Similarly, while reading a message from a file, Readln is used just as we used Writeln in the data entry file.

Here is a complete program to write a text message to a file.

```
Program Example (Input,Output) ;
Var
     Tfile : Text ;
     Contsent : Char ;
     Str255 : String ;
Begin
     Assign (Tfile, 'Pers.Doc') ;
     Rewrite (Tfile) ;
     Contsent := 'Y' ;
     While (Contsent='Y') do
       Begin
            Writeln ('Enter Message ') ;
            Readln(Str255) ;
            Writeln(Tfile,Str255) ;
            Writeln;
            Writeln('Want to Continue (Y/N) ') ;
            Readln(Contesent) ;
            Writeln;
         End;
Close(Tfile) ;
End.
```

Output

Enter Message

in the scenario of rapid innovation, fast changing technologies

Want to Continue (Y/N)
Y
Enter Message
and ever increasing application needs indian software professionals

Want to Continue (Y/N)
Y
Enter Message
can upgrade their skills to match the best in the world

Want to Continue (Y/N)
N

The following program which uses the text file entered by the above program is used to count number of vowels present in the file.

```
Program Example (Input,Output);
Var
     Tfile : Text ;
     Str255 : String;
     I,Na, Ne,Ni,No,Nu : Integer;
Begin
     Assign(Tfile,'Pers.Doc');
     Reset(Tfile);
     Na := O; Ne := O ; Ni : = O; No := O ; Nu := O;
     While Not Eof(Tfile) Do
         Begin
             Readln(Tfile,Str255);
             For I := 1 To Length(Str255) Do
                Begin
                    If (Str255(i) = 'a') Then Inc(Na);
                    If (Str255(i) = 'e') Then Inc(Ne);
                    If (Str255(i) = 'i') Then Inc(Ni);
                    If (Str255(i) = 'o') Then Inc(No);
                    If (Str255(i) = 'u') Then Inc(Nu);
                End;
         End;
     Writeln('Number of A''s ',Na);
     Writeln('Number of E''s ',Ne);
     Writeln('Number of I''s ',Ni);
     Writeln('Number of O''s ',No);
     Writeln('Number of U''s ',Nu);
Close (Tfile);
End.
```

Output

Number of A's 14
Number of E's 17
Number of I's 17
Number of O's 12
Number of U's 1

In the above illustration, the text in a file is read line by line using ReadIn. The For loop is used to count the vowels in every line. The function Length( ) is used to count the number of letters in a line. If the letter is found to be a vowel, the corresponding variable is incremented by one through inc( ) function. Thus the process repeats until all the lines in a file are read.

Few more examples regarding the text file will be seen in the solved problem section also.

RANDOM FILES

So far we have seen sequential access method in which all the records in a file are processed sequentially. There may be some instance where we want to process a particular record without disturbing the other records in a file. In such occasions, Random files are found to be most useful.

In this case, the normal procedure to open a file, close a file, write a record into a file and read a record from a file are the same as sequential access. The only difference is that before entering a record we must specify its record pointer, which of course is an integer. Only after entering the record pointer the information relevant to that record is fed. Similarly during processing, the record pointer for the record which we want to process is first entered. The corresponding record for that record pointer is read and then processed as per our requirements.

To read or to write a record in a file at any particular position we are using a standard procedure seek. The Syntax for this procedure is as follows.

```
Seek(file variable , Position) ;
```

Here, **file variable** is the typed binary file's variable (a file which contains non-printable characters). **Position** is an integer variable and also a record number to move the file variable.

The Example program consists of three fields and the structure is as follows.

```
Emprec = Record
              Empno : Integer ;
              EmpName : String ;
              Desgn : String ;
          End;
```

In this program we are using **EmpNo** as our record pointer.

```
Program Example(Input,Output);
Type
    Emprec = Record
                Empno : Integer ;
                EmpName : String ;
                Desgn : String ;
            End;
Var
    Empinfo : Emprec ;
    Empfile : File of Emprec;
    Yesno : Char ;
Begin
    Assign(Empfile,'Emp.Dat');
    Rewrite(Empfile);
    Yesno := 'Y' ;
    While (Yesno='Y') Do
     Begin
        With Empinfo Do
        Begin
            Write('Enter Employee Number : ');
            Readln(Empno);
            Seek(Empfile,Empno);
            Write('Enter Employee Name : ');
            Readln(EmpName);
            Write('Enter Designation : ');
            Readln(Desgn);
            Write(Empfile,Empinfo);
        End;
          Writeln;
          Write('Want To Continue (Y/N) : ');
          Readln(Yesno);
          Writeln;
    End;
    Close(Empfile);
End.
```

Output

Enter Employee Number	:	101
Enter Employee Name	:	Hussain
Enter Designation	:	System Programmer

Want To Continue (Y/N)	:	Y

Enter Employee Number	:	110
Enter Employee Name	:	Jayasankar
Enter Designation	:	System Analyst

Want To Continue (Y/N)	:	Y

Enter Employee Number	:	120
Enter Employee Name	:	Sabarjit
Enter Designation	:	Programmer

Want To Continue (Y/N)	:	N

Program file for accessing a particular record using *Empno* as key

```
Program Example(Input,Output);
Type
     Emprec = Record
          Empno     : Integer ;
          EmpName  : String ;
          Desgn    : String ;
          End;
Var
     Empinfo : Emprec ;
     Empfile : File of Emprec;
     Yesno   : Char ;
Begin
        Assign(Empfile,'Emp.Dat');
        Reset(Empfile);
        Yesno := 'Y' ;
        While (Yesno='Y') Do
        Begin
          Write('Enter Employee Number : ');
          Readln(Empinfo.Empno);
          Seek(Empfile,Empinfo.Empno);
          Read(Empfile,Empinfo);
```

```
                    Writeln('Employee Name : 'Empinfo.EmpName) ;
                    Writeln('Designation : ',Empinfo.Desgn) ;
                    Writeln;
                            Write('Want To Continue (Y/N) : ') ;
                            Readln(Yesno) ;
                            Writeln;
                    End;
                    Close(Empfile);
End.
```

Output

Enter Employee Number : 110
Employee Name : Jayasankar
Designation : System Analyst

Want To Continue (Y/N) : Y

Enter Employee Number : 101
Employee Name : Hussain
Designation : System Programmer

Want To Continue (Y/N) : N

UNTYPED BINARY FILES

Similar to that of the typed binary file, it is also possible to store data as an untyped binary file. Since this type of file does not have any specific data type, data can be read from and written to the file as a buffer. These untyped binary file stores information in buffer areas.

The method for creating such an untyped binary file is identical to the typed binary file. The general format for opening and closing a file is the same as that of a text file.

Here the file variable declared as 'File' that indicates it is an untyped file. The syntax for such declaration takes the following form.

```
        Var
            Identifier : File :
```

The identifier is the untyped binary file variable's name.

The next step is to specify whether the file has been opened for Reading or writing data to a file. This can be carried out by using a usual standard procedure such as **Rewrite** and **Reset** with slight modifications. The general form for Rewrite is as follows.

```
Rewrite (file variable, record size) ;
```
Here,

File variable is the variable opened for writing

and

record size is taken as 128 bytes if it is left blank. Otherwise we have to state the number of bytes to be written.

The syntax for the standard procedure Reset is similar to Rewrite and it is as follows.

```
Reset (file variable, record size) ;
```
Here,

File variable is the variable opened for reading data from a file and **Record size** is the amount of bytes to be read from the opened file and it considers 128 bytes if it is omitted.

Further we have to see how the read and write operations taken place in an untyped binary file. We are using two more standard procedures, Blockread and Blockwrite to carry out the said actions.

Blockwrite

The general form for Blockwrite is as follows.

```
Blockwrite (file var, buffer, number of records,
            number of records written) ;
```

Blockread

The general form for Blockread is as follows.

```
Blockread (file var, buffer, number of records,
           number of records read);
```

Here **file var** is an untyped file variable opened for Writing, **buffer** is any variable which is large enough to hold the block to be written. It is preferable to have a buffer as an array.

Number of records is the amount of records to write in **(Blockwrite)** and it is followed by actual number of records written to the file. Number of records is the amount of records to read (in **Blockread)** and it is followed by actual number of records read from the file.

To demonstrate the above features we have considered the following example program which copies the content of one file to another one.

```
Program Example(Input,Output);
Var
     Buffer : Array[1..1024] of char;
     Sfile,Tfile : File;
     Sfile1,Tfile1 : String;
     byteread,bytewrite : Integer ;
Begin
        Write ('Enter Source File Name : ');
        Readln(Sfile1);
        Write('Enter Target File Name : ');
        Readln(Tfile1);

        Assign(Sfile,Sfile1);
        Reset(Sfile,1);

        Assign(Tfile,Tfile1);
        Rewrite(Tfile,1);

     Repeat
          Blockread (Sfile, buffer,1024,byteread);
          Blockwrite(Tfile,buffer,byteread,bytewrite);
     Until(Byteread = 0) or (byteread <> bytewrite);
Close(Sfile);
Close(Tfile);
End.
```

Output

Enter Source File Name : 8ex1.Pas
Enter Target File Name : test.Pas

Note that in the procedures **Reset** and **Rewrite,** there is an extra entry followed by its file reference. This extra argument is called the record size for the untyped binary file and it is optional. If it is omitted, a default record size (128) will be taken for the untyped binary file.

To verify, whether the source file has been copied into target file, type the target file against the **DOS** prompt.

Some advanced file handling commands can also be seen in the solved problem sections.

Passing a file variable as a parameter to procedure

Though the title may sound strange, it is somewhat similar to passing an ordinary variable to a procedure. This enables the programmer to write procedures that redirect both input and output.

The only difference from the ordinary variable is, in the procedure the file variable is declared as a variable parameter.

Here is an example program to explore the concept of passing of file variable to a procedure.

```
Program Example (Input,Output) ;
Type
     Watchrec = Record
                      Make : String ;
                      Model : String ;
                      Price : Integer ;
                   End;
     Watchfile = File of Watchrec;
Var
     Wrec : Watchrec;
     Wfile : Watchfile;
Procedure Getrecord (Var Wfile1 : Watchfile ;
                         Wrec1 : Watchrec);
Var
     Yesno : Char ;
Begin
     Yesno := 'Y' ;
     While (Yesno = 'Y') do
         Begin
             With Wrec1 do
                 Begin
                     Write ('Enter Brand Name : ');
                     Readln(Make) ;
                     Write('Model Name : ');
                     Readln(Model) ;
                     Write('Price: ');
                     Readln(Price) ;
                     Write(Wfile1,Wrec1);
                 End;
             Writeln;
             Write('Want To Continue [Y/N] ');
             Readln(Yesno);
```

```
            End;
    End;

    {Main Starts}

    Begin
            Assign(Wfile,Watch.Dat ');
            Rewrite(Wfile);
            Getrecord(Wfile,Wrec);
            Close(Wfile);
    End.
```

Output

Enter Brand Name	: HMT
Model Name	: Vijay
Price	: 450

Want To Continue   (Y/N)Y

Enter Brand Name	: Titan
Model Name	: Classique
Price	: 1100

Want To Continue   (Y/N)Y

Enter Brand Name	: Timex
Model Name	: Aquara
Price	: 800

Want to Continue   (Y/N) N

Exercises

1. Differentiate sequential access and direct access of a file.

2. What are the advantages of a sequential data file compared with a random data file?

3. What is a text file in PASCAL? Illustrate with examples.

4. Write a program to create 2 files, one to store odd numbers and another to store even numbers in the range 1-100.

5. Write a Pascal program to create sequential data file with the following informations. Player name, Team name, Batting average. Using this data file, write another program to print a teamwise list containing names of players with their batting average.

6. Write a function to convert all lower case English to upper case letters in a file.

7. A data file contains the following details

   Name of Student   30 chars

   Register number   Integer

   Marks in Mathematics,   Integer
   Physics, Chemistry

   declare an appropriate structure and process the file to get the print out of Register number, Name, Marks in Mathematics, Physics, Chemistry and the average of the three marks. Also find the number of students who have scored less than 40, 40 to 60 and above 60 on the average.

8. Write a function to find the length of each line of input and find the average length of a line in a given text file.

9. A hospital keeps a file of blood donors in which each record has the form

   Name   String[30]

   Address   String[40]

   Age   Integer

   Blood group   Char [A,B,O]

i)   Write a program to create a data file for N blood donors.

ii) Use the data file to print out all the blood donors whose age is below 35 and blood is of 'O' type.

10. Develop a Pascal Program that would create a file to process student's mark list. How do you append a new record into a sequential file.

11. Explain the file associated statements used in Pascal with examples.

12. Write a Pascal program that produces total marks for each student and overall class average from a student's file containing student number, 5 subjects marks for each student.

13. A disk file STUDENT.DAT contains records of various students. Each student record consists of register number "91-CS-0001" to "91-CS-0099", name first and last separately, each having not more than 30 chars, marks of 5 different subjects as integers. Write a PASCAL program to read STUDENT.DAT file and to display the contents with total and pass status.

14. Write a PASCAL program to create sequential variable record size file "EMPLOYEE.INF" having appropriate fields such as EMPNO,EMP-NAME,MARRIED-STATUS. If MARRIED-STATUS = 'YES' then PARTNER-NAME, DATE-MARRIED, CHILDREN, should be given as input.

15. Write a program to create a text file and copy the contents of this file to another file.

16. Write a program which will read a text file and count all occurrences of a particular word.

17. A file "marks.int" is a data file defined as an integer type. It contains the marks of 10 students. Read this file and find the average marks. Also write a program to append a file.

SOLVED PROBLEMS

1. If the data to a program file is

Rama 101

Anumar 105

Rama 101

Kosalai 103

Kaikegi 104

Anumar 105

Rama 101

Dhasarathan 109

Bharathan 108

Lakshmanan 107

Write a sequential file to eliminate the duplicate records. The name of the input file is **'Sort .Dat'**. The output should be written to another file in the name of **'Sort1.Dat'**.

```
Program Example (Input,Output);
Type
        Stdrec = Record
           Name : String[20];
           No : Integer ;
        End;
Var
    Markrec : Array [1..10] of Stdrec;
    Temp : Stdrec;
    SortFile, SortOutFile : File of Stdrec;
    I,N,J : Integer;
Begin
    Assign(Sortfile, 'Sort.Dat');
    Reset(SortFile);
    Assign(SortOutFile, 'Sort1.Dat');
    Rewrite(SortOutFile);
    N:=0;
    While Not Eof(Sortfile) do
      Begin
        N:=N+1;
           With martkrec[N] do
              Read(SortFile,Markrec[N]) ;
        End;
```

```
           For I :=1 to N-1 do
                For J:=I+1 to N do
                    If (Markrec[I].No > Markrec[J]. No) then
                       Begin
                          Temp:=Markrec[I];
                          Markrec[I] :=Markrec[J];
                          Markrec[J] :=Temp;
                       End;
For I:=1 to N-1 do
     If (Markrec [I].No < > Markrec [I+1].No) then
     Begin
        Write (SortOutFile,Markrec[I] );
        Writeln (Markrec[I].Name:20 Markrec[I].No:10);
     End;
Write (SortOutFile,Markrec[I] );
Close (SortFile) ;
Close (SortOutFile) ;
End.
```

Output

Rama 101
Kosalai 103
Kaikegi 104
Anumar 105
Lakshmanan 107
Bharathan 108

2. Write a Pascal program to find a particular character and replace
    every occurrence of it by another character. [Replace o with a]

Input File Contains

Oracle is one of the most exciting programs for microcomputers
systems on the market today.

```
Program Example;
Var
     Filel, File2 : Text;
     FindChar, RepChar : Char;
     Str80 : String;
     I : Integer;
Begin
```

```
Assign (File1, 'File.Txt') ;
Reset (File1) ;
Assign (File2, 'File1.txt');
Rewrite (File2) ;
Writeln ('Enter Find Char ');
Readln(FindChar) ;
Writeln ('Replace with ') ;
Readln (Repchar) ;
While Not Eof (File1) do
        Begin
            Readln(File1,Str80) ;
            For I :=1 to Length (Str80) do
            If (Str80[I] =FindChar) then
               Write (File2,Repchar)
            Else
               Write(File2,Str80[I]);
            Writeln(File2, ' ') ;
        End;
    Close(File1) ;
    Close(file2) ;
End.
```

Output

Enter Find Char
o
Replace With
a

Output file :

**Oracle is one of the mast exciting programs
for microcamputers systems in the market today.**

3.   Program to beautify the text file, by giving left and right margins.

{PROGRAM TO SET THE MARGINS OF THE GIVEN TEXT}

```
Program Margin (Input,Output);
Uses Crt;
Var
    F1, F2 : Text;
    Fname1, Fname2, Line, Tok, Temp : String;
```

```pascal
    Token : Array [1..100] of string;
    I, J, I1, I2, K, Len, Le, 1, Lm, Rm : Integer;
Begin
    Clrscr;
    Write ('Enter the input file name : ') ;
    Readln (Fname1) ;
    Assign (F1, Fname1) ;
    Reset (F1) ;
    Write ('Enter the output file name : ') ;
    Readln (Fname2) ;
    Assign (F2, Fname2) ;
    Rewrite (F2) ;
    Write ('Enter the left margin value : ') ;
    Readln (Lm) ;
    Write ('Enter the right margin value : ') ;
    Readln (Rm) ;
    For I1 := 1 to Lm do
            Write (F2,' ') ;
    L := Lm;
    While not eof (F1) do
    Begin
      J := 0;
      I := 1;
      Readln (F1, line) ;
      Line := Line + ' ' ;
      Len := Length (Line) ;
      While (I < len ) do
        Begin
          Tok := ' ' ;
          While (line[I] <> ' ') and (line[I] <>
                                      char (13) ) do
          Begin
            Tok := Tok + Line[I] ;
            I := I + 1;
          End;
            If line[I] = char (13) then I := I + 1;
            While line[I] = ' 'do
            Begin
              I := I + 1;
              J := J + 1;
              Token[J] := Tok;
            End;
            For K := 1 to J do .
```

```
            Begin
               Le := Length(Token[K] )
               If e <= (rm-1) then
        Begin
           Write (F2, Token[k] ) ;
           Write (F2, '  ') ;
           l :=   le+l+1;
        End
        Else
           Begin
              Writeln (F2) ;
              Write (F2, '  ' : lm) ;
              l := lm;
              Write (F2, Token [K]) ;
              Write (F2, '  ') ;
              l := l+lm+1;
              End;
           End;
    End;
Writeln ('******* margin setting is completed ******** ' );
Close(F1) ;
Close(F2) ;
End.
```

Output

Enter the input file name : TEST

Enter the output file name : TEST1

Enter the left margin value : 10

Enter the right margin value : 50

************ margin setting is completed **********

Input File

Unlike the US and many other advanced countries, India
does not use many computers, so the amount of energy saves
through Energy star systems will be less here. Moreover unlike US,
Where 90 percent of the pc's run 24 hours. In India only 25
percent of the pc's run 24 hours, most of them being
BBSes, networks, etc.

Output File.

Unlike the US and many other advanced
countries, India does not use many
computers, so the amount of energy saves
through Energy star systems will be
less here. Moreover unlike US,
where 90 percent of the pc's run
24 hours. In India only 25
percent of the pc's run 24 hours,
most of them being BBSes,
networks, etc.

Chapter – 9

USER DEFINED DATA TYPES, SETS AND UNITS

We have already seen in the second chapter that the standard type has two branches viz., Simple type data and user defined data type. Also, in Procedures and Function we have abundantly used user defined data type to pass an array to Procedures and Functions.

In this chapter, we will explore some of the advanced topics in the user defined data types. The user defined data type is further divided into Enumerated data type and Subrange. We shall explain them one by one in detail.

Enumerated Data Type

The items given in a particular order is called Enum. The value in the list starts from **0** to **n–1**, where **n** is the total number of items given in the list. Consider the following example

```
Type
        Brand = (Nexus, Dcm, Hcl, Siva);
Var
        Computer : Brand;
```

In the above case, we have 4 items in the list. Each item in the list can be accessed by subtracting one from the positional value of an identifier.

Advantage of using the above type is that we referenced the members in computer type by giving the name of the computer.

```
Program Example (Input, Output);
Type
   Brand = (Nexus, Dcm, Hcl, Siva);
Var
   Computer : Brand;
Begin
    Computer := Nexus;
    Case Computer of
        Nexus : Writeln ('Well known for LAN ' );
        Dcm :  Writeln (' Best in Mini Computers ');
        Hcl :  Writeln (' Famous for its Busybee systems ');
        Siva : Writeln (' Dominating PC field ');
    Else
```

```
    Writeln ('Given system not found in the library ');
  End;
End.
```

Output

Well Known for LAN

As there is no input and output statement associated with this type, the brand name 'Nexus' is assigned to Computer.

Subrange

We know that an integer data type allows the range from −32768 to +32767. For instance, if we want to enter numbers between 1 to 100 for an integer variable, it is likely that the user may enter numbers which are out of the range also. To restrict the user from entering numbers other than those within the specified range, subrange is used. Thus subrange data type is very useful in data validation.

The method of defining a subrange is as follows :

```
Type
        Mark = 1..100;
Var
        S1, S2, S3 : Mark;
```

The integer variable S1, S2 and S3 will take only integer numbers that fall between 1 to 100. It gives a runtime error, if we attempt to give a mark that lies outside the specified range.

Here is a program, to clarify the above concept.

```
{$r+}
Program Example (Input,Output);
Type
        Mark = 1..100;
Var
        S1, S2, S3 : Mark;
        Tot : Integer ;
Begin
        Writeln('Enter 3 Marks ');
        Readln(S1,S2,S3);
        Tot := S1 + S2 + S3 ;
        Writeln ('Total Marks : ',Tot);
End.
```

Output

Enter 3 Marks
34 55 333
Runtime error 201 at 1DEF:0084.

Enter 3 Marks
34 44 55
Total Marks : 133

In the above program, we have noticed the change in the very first line, i.e., we have introduced a symbol {$r+} and it is called as compiler directive. It is used here for range checking purposes, so that the user is protected from entering numbers other than those within the specified range.

SETS

To make Pascal a distinguished language among all high level languages, the developers of Pascal have adorned it with yet another branch in structured data type called SETS. A Pascal SET is a collection of elements, and is formed by combining members of an ordinal data type or Subrange of ordinal data type, and it is very much similar to a set in mathematics.

We can declare Pascal set either through type declaration or through Var statement.

* To declare a set data type through type declaration

```
Type
        Identifier = Set of ordinal data type ;
```

* To declare a set data type through var statement

```
Var
        Identifier : Set of Ordinal data type ;
```

Here, Identifier is the usual data type identifier. The Set of ordinal data type is also called as base type. It may be an integer, real, char, boolean or a user defined data type. Now we will see how a set may be defined.

To create a set of numeric digits from 0 to 10 the following declaration may be used.

```
Type
        No0to10 = Set of 0..10;
```

To create a set of characters comprising vowels, the declaration is

```
Type
    Vowels = Set of ('A', 'a', 'E', 'e', 'I', 'i', 'O', 'o', 'U', 'u');
```

From the above declarations it is seen that the elements in a set must be drawn from the same base type.

Set Operators

The following is a list of set operators that are operated with the same base type.

+ Union

− Difference

* Intersection

The Pascal set union operator (+) returns the result that contains the elements of one set expression with the elements of another set expression.

The syntax for using Union operator is

```
Set expression + set expression
```

For example

Set A Contains the elements a, b, c, d and e. Set B contains the elements b, c, d, e, f and g. On performing the Union operator, the resultant SetC contains a, b, c, d, e, f and g.

The Pascal set difference operator (−) returns the result that contains elements of a second set expression removed from a first set expression.

The syntax for using Difference operator is

```
set expression - set expression
```

For example SetA contains the elements a, b, c, d, e and SetB contains the elements b, c, d, e, f, g then the resultant set, SetC will have only 'a' as its element.

The Pascal set intersection operator (*) returns a set of elements, that are formed by combining common elements from both of the set expressions, on which it is operated.

The syntax for using Intersection operator is

>   set expression * set expression

For example, let SetC contains the elements a,b,c and SetB contains the elements b, c, d, e, f. The resultant set of SetC* SetB will take b and c as it is common to both the sets.

The following example program will demonstrate the usage of all the above set operators in a complete manner.

```
Program Example(Input,Output);
Type
        Lowcase = 'a' .. 'z';
        Setofchar = set of Lowcase ;
Var
        SetA, SetB, SetC, SetD : Setofchar;
Procedure Writeset (Charin : Setofchar);
Var
        Charindex : Char;
Begin
        For Charindex := 'a' to 'z' do
        if (charindex in charin) then

                Write (Charindex :3);
        Writeln;

End;

{Main Starts}

Begin
        SetA := ['a' .. 'e'];
        SetB := ['b' .. 'g'];
        SetC := ['a' .. 'c'];
        SetD := ['b' .. 'f'];
        Writeln ('Set Union Operation (+) ');
        Writeset (SetA+SetB);
        Writeln ('Set Union Operation (-) ');
        Writeset (SetA-SetB);
        Writeln ('Set Union Operation (*) ');
        Writeset (SetC*SetD);
End.
```

Output

Set Union Operation (+)
   a b c d e f g

Set Subtraction Operation (–)
   a

Set Intersection Operation (*)
   b c

In the above example, we have used a procedure **Writeset** to point the resultant of set operation, since, Turbo Pascal does not support any standard procedure to print the set type values.

The following is a list of Pascal set operators that can be used to compare sets in boolean expression.

   =   Equals

   <>.   Not equals

   >=   Is a superset of (Set greater than or equal to)

   <=   Is a subset of (Set less than or equal to)_

   IN   Membership of

The 'Set equal to' operator (=) returns either true or false upon comparison. The resultant will be true if two set expressions are equal, otherwise the **set equal to** operator returns false.

The syntax for using 'set equal to' operator is

```
Boolean Identifier := set expression = set expression;
```

The 'Set not equal to' operator (<>) returns true if the set expressions are not equal with one another. If the set expressions are equal in value, the 'set not equal to' operator returns false.

The syntax for using 'set not equal to' operator is

```
Boolean Identifier := set expression <> set expression :
```

The Pascal 'set greater than or equal to' operator (>=) returns true if the first set contains all the elements which are present in the second set expression also. Otherwise, the Pascal **set greater than or equal to'** operator returns false.

The syntax for using Pascal 'set greater than or equal to' operator is

```
Boolean Identifier := set expression >= set expression ;
```

The Pascal **'set less than or equal to'** operator (<=) returns true if all elements in the second set expression, contains the elements of first set expression. Otherwise, the Pascal **'set less than or equal to'** operator returns false.

The syntax for using Pascal **set less than or equal to** operator is

Boolean Identifier := set expression <= set expression;

The following program demonstrates the usage of set comparison operators in detail.

```
Program Example(Input,Output);
Type
          Lowcase = 'a' .. 'z' ;
          Setofchar = Set of Lowcase;
Var
          SetA, SetB, SetC, SetD : Set of char;
  Begin
    SetA := ['a' .. 'e'];
    SetB := ['b' .. 'g'];
    SetC := ['a' .. 'c'];
    SetD := ['b' .. 'f'];
    Writeln ('Set Equal to Operation (=) SetA=SetB is ');
    Writeln (SetA=SetB);
    Writeln ('Set Not Equal to Operation (<>) SetA<>=SetB is ');
    Writeln (SetA<>SetB);
    Writeln ('Set Greater than or Equal to Operation (>=) SetD>=SetB is');
    Writeln (SetD>=SetB);
    Writeln ('Set Less than or Equal to Operation (<=) SetB<=SetD is ');
    Writeln (SetB <= SetD);
  End.
```

Output

**Set Equal to Operation (=) SetA=SetB is
FALSE
Set Not Equal to Operation (<>) SetA<>SetB is
TRUE**

Set Greater than or Equal to Operation (>=) SetD >=SetB is FALSE
Set Less than or Equal to Operation (<=) SetB <= SetD is FALSE

The Pascal set **IN** operator returns true if the ordinal value is contained in the set. Otherwise. Set **IN** operator returns false.

The syntax for using Pascal set **IN** operator is

```
Ordinal expression IN set expression
```

Let us understand the **IN** operator by executing the following program. The program is developed to count the number of vowels in a given string.

```
Program Example (Input,Output);
Type
     Capital letter = 'A'..'Z' ;
     Setofchar = set of capital letter;
Var
     Str80 : String;
     NoOfVow,Index : Integer;
     UpVowels : Setofchar;
Begin
     UpVowels :=['A', 'E', 'I', 'O', 'U',];
     Writeln ('Enter string');
     Readln (Str80);
     NoOfVow := 0 ;
     For Index :=1 to Length(str80) do
     If (upcase(str80[index]) in upvowels)then
        Inc (NoOfVow);
     Writeln('No of Vowels present in the given string is',NoOfVow);
End.
```

Output

Enter String
Who says you can't win them all?
No of Vowels present in the given string is 8

The user is liable to enter both upper case and lower case vowels in a string and consequently it becomes necessary to test both the cases. In order to avoid this difficulty, we first convert a character into an upper case character by using a character function **Upcase( )** and then the checking takes place. By the above method, we have avoided double checking. We have used **INC( )** function to increment the number of vowels by one.

UNITS

The good old programmers of Turbo Pascal finds it an embellishment to the new version. They find it very difficult to repeat certain set of programming code in their program, as it makes the program too lengthy. It is also a very tedious job to debug such programs.

One way of alleviating the above problem is to write procedures and functions. Note that inclusion of such procedures and functions will only reduce the repeated coding in a particular program where it appears. Assume that there are number of programmers who are using the same set of coding for a particular task in their programs. Then each one has to incorporate the same code in their program.

The other way is by writing the same code only once and making it available as a global one. Such an arrangement can be accomplished by using UNITS.

Turbo Pascal also provides some of the procedures through its units.

For example, if we want to clear the screen, we have to include a unit called CRT, in which there is a procedure called **clrscr**, using which we can clear the screen. Similarly, for positioning the text message on the screen, the same unit provides us with yet another procedure, by name **gotoxy( )**. Also we have directed our output only to the screen; if we want to pass our result to the printer, then we have to include another unit called PRINTER. We shall see how these units can be invoked in our program.

In Pascal, there is a keyword **USES**, to activate the specific unit. It is placed immediately after the program header and the general form is as follows :

```
USES
        Unitnames;
```

for example,

```
Uses
        CRT, PRINTER;
```

We can also include more than one unit in the same program and separate them by commas as shown above.

Now we shall focus our attention on how to develop similar units to facilitate our programming.

The structure of any Pascal Unit takes the following form

```
UNIT Unitnames;

Interface

          Procedure headings and function headings

Implementation

          Source code procedure and function

Begin
          Initialisation code

End.
```

The entire unit can be involved just by referring its unit name. It follows the interface, here we can declare variables, constants and prototypes of procedures and functions which take part in the main program.

The penultimate section of a unit is implementation. Here, we can declare any variables and other data type, that would not be available to the main program. It is also used to include procedures and functions both as private and public.

The last section of a Pascal unit is the initialisation code. In this, we are using period (.) instead of semicolon (;) to end the initialisation code.

The following example unit is, to display a message in a particular location. Let us see how a unit can be created, compiled and executed.

Type the following program in the editor :

```
Unit Unit1;
Interface
   Procedure Writemessxy(X,Y : Integer ; Givstring : String);
Implementation
Uses CRT;
          Procedure Writemessxy ;
          Begin

               Gotoxy (x,y);
               Write (Givstring);
          End;
Begin
End.
```

Now compile the above program and save it by name **'UNIT1.PAS',** After getting **"Success Press any Key"** message, select the destination option from the compilation menu. Now by pressing 'enter' key, change the destination from disk to memory. Recompile the above program to get a new unit in the name of **UNIT1.TPU.**

To test the above unit, type the following program and run it.

```
Program Example (Input,output);
Uses Unit1;
Begin
     Writemessxy (10,4, 'Welcome To Turbo Pascal');
End.
```

Similar units can be created to get more aquaintance with the units.

Redirecting Output to Printer

To redirect output to printer we have to use the standard unit Printer in the uses statement.

The Printer unit contains predefined support for working with a printer.

Consider the following program example which redirect its output to printer.

```
Program Example(Input, Output);
Uses
   Printer ;
Var
   I : Integer ;
Begin
   For I := 1 to 5 do

     Writeln (lst, 'Welcome To Turbo Pascal Version 5.5 ');
End.
```

Here, Writeln is followed by **'Lst'** which denotes the printer device. Instead of passing output to default output device i.e. to screen here we are passing output to printer. To get the output for the above program execute the program with printer turned on.

CHAPTER - 10

POINTERS

Pointer data type is perhaps the most important and advanced topic of this book. Readers who are familiar with BASIC and FORTRAN often find this topic to be a strange one. A pointer is nothing but a variable which stores the address of another variable. The variable we have declared in the declaration part will have a unique address in the memory. So far, we have not bothered about the addresses of these variables. In this topic we are taking into account, the addresses of memory variables to extract the fullest capacity of Turbo Pascal.

First of all let us see the advantages of using pointers. For example, arrays and pointer data type have a close relationship with one another. Assume that a linear array is having 10 elements and we want to insert a new element in the middle of the list. Then we have to shift all the elements by one position till the desired position is reached as we did in Chapter 5. Ofcourse it is fairly simple if we have less number of elements in an array. Imagine a situation where we are having elements of the order of thousands. In that case shifting will take a lot of time and also it will not be considered as a good algorithm.

Another difficulty which we face during the array manipulation is, that the size of an array is fixed and it cannot be varied according to our wish. These shortcomings are overriden by using pointers, the topic on which we are focusing our concentration at present.

Pointers are used in building more complex data structures like linked lists, stacks, queues and binary trees. Unlike files and arrays these complex data structures can increase or decrease in size. The maximum size of such data structures need not be declared. A pointer variable is capable of having the address of a dynamic variable. Here dynamic means, the memory space of the variable allocated during the execution time.

Declaration of Pointer Variable

Like all other variables the pointer variable also needs to be declared well before it takes any action. To declare a pointer the character (circumflex or caret) is used. The following general form is used for declaration of pointers.

```
Var
Identifier : ^data type ;
```

We can explain the above through an example,

```
Var
        Ptr1 : ^Integer;
```

Here Ptr1 is a pointer to an integer. This value may be stored in memory somewhere.

Singly Linked List

In singly linked list each node has atleast one data field and address field (or link field). The address field contains the address of the next node in the structure.

Let us consider the following linked list structure:

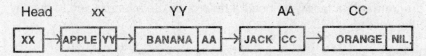

Head pointer points to the first node in the linked list. The link field of the last node has a **NIL** in it, to signify that it points to none. we can access any node provided we know the location of the first node. Whenever head = NIL, we say that the list is empty.

To insert a new node

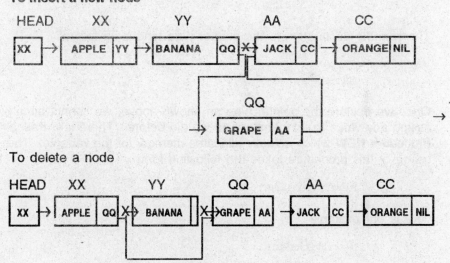

To delete a node

To explore the concept of Pointers, we are considering a linked list problem and it can be made by records and pointers. In linked list, as the name suggests, it has a link to the next data item in the chain. Linked list is very useful in situation where we don't know the amount of storage required by the linear array well in advance. In linked list we can easily insert and delete items without modifying the entire structure. Linked list can be constructed as singly, doubly and circularly linked list. In a singly linked list as we have already seen, there is one link to the next item, whereas in a doubly linked list there are two links one pointing to the previous item and another pointing to the next item. The use of these two will depend on the application intended.

We consider a singly linked list which consists of name examno and link as its elements. By using the above record we are going to construct a program with a facility to insert a record, delete a record and to display all the records.

The declaration for the above record is as follows :

```
Type
          Iyear = ^stdrec;
          Stdrec = Record
                      Name    : String;
                      ExamNo  : Integer;
                      Link    : Iyear;
                   End;
```

The variable declaration to the pointer data type is as follows :

```
Var
          Markrec : Iyear;
```

Once we declare the pointer type as shown above, we cannot simply assign any value to its members as we did before. There is a Pascal Procedure **NEW** which actually allocates memory for the variable. The usage of this procedure takes the following form

```
          new (Varname);
```

here is our example

```
          New(Markrec);
```

Now we can assign values to the members of the record in the usual method.

```
Markrec^.Name := 'Nikalus Wirth';
Markrec^.ExamNo := 1234 ;
```

The above can also be rewritten by using with structure to ease the coding as shown below.

```
With Markrec^ do
Begin
     Name : = 'Nikalus Wirth';
   ExamNo : = '1234';
End;
```

Turbo Pascal provides another reserved word NIL which should be used when all the elements are added to the list, the link field of the last record should be assigned this value.

```
Markrec^.Link := Nil ;
```

thus not leaving the link field of the last record abruptly.

Now let us first develop a procedure to insert a record.

```
Procedure InsertRecord(Var Markrec : Iyear);
Var
     Front,Rear, Next : Iyear ;
     Present : Boolean ;
Begin
     New(Front);
     Write('Enter Examno : ');
     Readln(Front^.ExamNo);
     Write (' Name : ');
     Readln(Front^.Name);
     Rear := Nil ;
     Next := Markrec ;
     Present := False ;
     while (Next <> Nil ) and Not Present do
        If ( Next^.Examno > Front^.Examno ) then
             Present := True
     Else
        Begin
          Rear := next ;
          Next := Next^.Link;
        End;
     Front^.Link := Next ;
```

```
If Rear = Nil then
   Markrec := Front
Else
   Rear^.Link := Front ;
End;
```

To begin with, the procedure creates a memory location for **Front** by using a predeclared procedure **New**. After allocating the memory location the user has to enter **Examno** and **Name** for the corresponding record. Now the procedure scans the linked list until an examno is found that is greater than the examno to be inserted. Since there is no record in the linked list initially the pointer Rear is initialised to Nil. Also our program has a facility to insert a record both at the beginning and at the end. Assuming that there will not be any record in the list when the procedure Insert Record is invoked at first. So, the Next pointer is set to point the markrec of the list.

Moreover, our program should monitor whether the examno is greater than the examno to be added has been found. To make room for this provision we are initialising False to the boolean variable present in the beginning.

Now the while loop is used to traverse the entire list and the loop terminates only when the following conditions are satisfied. When the end of the list has been attained, Next is initialised to Nil. Also the loop will terminate if the place for the insertion has been found within the list by making present to be true.

Before completing the loop, the following assignments have to be done.

Firstly, the Rear should point the element before the added element.

Secondly, Next should point the element after the added element.

So far, we have not made any provision to add an element as first element of the list. There are two options infront of us to do the above task. Either by modifying the pointer markrec or by modifying the link pointer of previous element in the list. Also note that the value of the rear was set to Nil at the beginning of the search. Suppose the inserted element is the first element of the list then the value of Rear is set to Nil at the end of the search.

Now let us develop a procedure to delete a record from a linked list.

Here the procedure **DISPOSE** is used to release the heap space taken up by a dynamic variable when it is no longer needed.

```
Procedure DeleteRecord(Var Markrec : Iyear);
Var
     Rear,Next :  Iyear ;
     TempExamNo : Integer ;
     Present : Boolean ;
Begin
        Write ('Enter ExamNo To delete ');
        Readln(TempExamNo);
        If (Markrec^.ExamNo = TempExamNo )Then
            Markrec := markrec^.Link
        Else
          Begin

                Rear := markrec ;
                next := Markrec^.Link;
                Present := False ;
                While (Next <> Nil ) and Not Present do
                  Begin
                  If (Next^.ExamNo = TempExamNo) Then
                    Begin
                        Present := True ;
                        Rear^.Link := Next^.Link;
                    End
                  Else
                    Begin
                        Rear := Next ;
                        Next := Next^.Link;
                    End;
               End;
          End;
        Dispose(Markrec);
End;
```

After receiving the Examno to be deleted from the linked list, we have to locate the position of the element to be deleted.

Suppose if we want to delete the first element of the linked list. It is to be checked first. If our choice is not the first element, then we have to initialize the pointer Rear to the markrec. Note the pointer Next is assigned the value of the pointer of the first element in the list.

A while loop is used to traverse the entire list to locate the position for deletion so as to change the links. In case if we enter the Examno which is not found in the linked list, we should exit from procedure without doing anything. For accomplishing this, we are using a boolean variable

(Present) to monitor whether the given examno is there or not. If the given Examno is not in the list, the boolean variable (Present) never attains true and the while loop exits when next equals nil.

Finally let us develop a procedure to traverse the Linked list.

```
Procedure DisplayRecord (markrec : Iyear );
Begin
        Writeln;
        While (Markrec<> Nil )do
          Begin
            Writeln('ExamNo: ',Markrec^.Examno);
            Writeln('name: ',Markrec^.name);
            Writeln;
            Markrec := Markrec^.Link ;
          End;
End;
```

Printing records in a linked list is very simple. Here we are using a while loop to print the records in the list. The while loop will terminate if markrec is equal to nil, which means that all the records in the linked list are printed.

Thus we have seen all the fundamental pointer operations involved in the linked list.

Implementation of Stacks using linked List

Stack, the **LIFO** data structure can be implemented by means of linked list. Stack pointer always points to the top most node in the stack

STACK POINTER

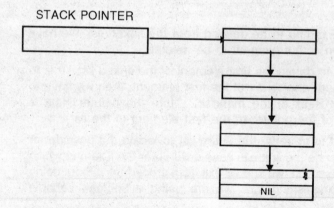

2 INITIALLY

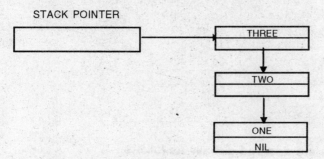

STACK POINTER

3 AFTER A PUSH OPERATION

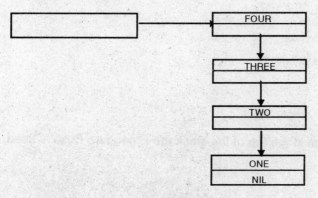

STACK POINTER

4 AFTER A POP OPERATION

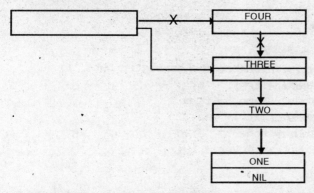

STACK POINTER

The following program illustrates the stack operations. The maximum stack size is initialised as 5 and the declaration is as follows.

```
Const
     MaxStackSize = 5;
Type
     Sptr =^Sdata ;
     Sdata = Record
           SName : String;
           Next : Sptr ;
           End;
```

Here the variables are declared globally as follows :

```
Var
     Top,VPtr,Node : Sptr;
     Res,Item : String;
     Choice,Count : Integer;
     Stack : Sdata;
```

Initially in the main program

Top := Nil;

Which signifies an empty stack.

To insert a new item in the top of the stack the Procedure Push is used.

```
Procedure Push ;
Begin
     If (Count = MaxStackSize) Then
           Begin
                 Writeln('Stack full');
                 Writeln('Data cannot be pushed further');
           End
     Else
           Begin
                 New(Node);
                 Writeln('Enter the character Data ');
                 Readln(Item);
                 Node^.SName := Item ;
                 Node^.next := Top ;
                 Top := Node;
                 Count := Count + 1 ;
           End;
End;
```

Whenever the Procedure Push is called a new node is created and it is made as the top node of the stack. The link field of the new node is made to point to the previously created node. The top pointer always points to the top most element of the stack.

This procedure handles the condition for stack overflow (Stack Full). After each Push operation the variable Count is incremented by 1. When Count becomes equal to maxStackSize, Stack overflow condition occurs. After this elements cannot be pushed further.

To delete an element from the Top of the stack the Procedure Pop is used.

```
Procedure Pop;
Begin
If (Top <> Nil) Then
        Begin
                Item : =Top^,Sname ;
                Writeln('Popped Data;', Item);
                Node := Top ;
                Top   := Top^,Next;
                Dispose(node);
                Count := Count - 1 ;
        End
    Else
        Begin
                Writeln('Data cannot be Popped ');
                WrireIn('Empty Stack');
        End;
End;
```

Another temporary pointer is used to point to the topmost element to be disposed. Then the top is made to point to the next node in the stack and count is decremented by 1.

i.e.,

```
Top := Top^.Next ;
```

The temporary pointer is disposed to return the memory occupied by the deleted node, when Top points to Nil or Count=0 stack underflow (stack empty) condition occurs. When stack empty condition is reached further Pop operation cannot be performed.

To View the contents of the LIFO structure Procedure View is used.

```
Procedure View;
Begin
    CIrscr;
    Vptr := Top;
    If (Top = nil ) Then
      Writeln('Empty Stack')
    Else
      Begin
        While (Vptr <> Nil) Do
            Begin
                Item := Vptr^.Sname ;
                Writeln(Item);
                Vptr := Vptr^.Next ;
            End;
        End;
End;
```

The complete program is presented below.

```
Program Example(Input, Output);
Uses Crt;
Const
    MaxStackSize = 5;
Type
    Sptr =^Sdata ;

    Sdata = Record
        SName : String;
        Next : Sptr;
        End;
Var
    Top,VPtr,Node : Sptr;
    Res,Item : String;
    Choice,Count : Integer;
    Stack : Sdata;
Procedure Push ;
    Begin
        If (Count = MaxStackSize ) Then
        Begin
            Writeln ('Stack Full');
            Writeln('Data cannot be pushed further');
        End
```

```
                Else
                Begin
                      New(Node);
                      Writeln('Enter the Character Data ');
                      Readln(Item);
                      Node^.SName := Item ;
                      Node^.Next := Top;
                      Top := Node ;
                      Count := Count + 1 ;
                End;
          End;

Procedure pop;
      Begin
            If (Top <> Nil ) Then
                Begin
                   item := Top^.Sname;
                   Writeln ('PoPPed data : ',Item);
                   Node := Top;
                   Top := Top^.Next ;
                   Dispose(Node) ;
                   Count := Count - 1 ;
                End
        Else
            Begin
                  Writeln('Data cannot be Popped ');
                  Writeln('Empty Stack ');
            End;
      End;


Procedure View ;

Begin
      Clrscr;
      Vptr := Top;
      If ( Top = Nil ) Then
          Writeln ('Empty Stack ')
      Else
          Begin
            While (Vptr <> Nil ) Do
                  Begin
                      Item := Vptr^.Sname ;
                      Writeln(Item);
```

```
                    Vptr := Vptr^.Next ;
                End;
            End;

{Main Program Starts}

Begin
  Count := 0;
  Top := Nil ;
  Repeat
    Clrscr ;
    Writeln('Linked List Implementation of Stack ');
    Writeln('1. push ');
    Writeln;
    Writeln('2. pop ');
    Writeln;
    Writeln('3. View ');
    Writeln;
    Writeln('4.Exit ');
    Writeln;
    Readln(Choice);

                Case choice of
                    1:
                        Begin
                          Clrscr:
                          Writeln ('Push Operation');
                          Push;
                        End;

                    2:
                        Begin
                          Clrscr:
                          Writeln ('Pop Operation');
                          Pop;
                        End;

                    3:
                        Begin
                          Clrscr:
                          Writeln ('View Operation');
                          View;
                        End;
```

```
4:
        Begin
            Clrscr:
            Exit;
        End;
    End;

    Writeln('Want To continue [Y/N] ');
    Readln(Res);
Until (Res= 'N');
End.
```

For output execute the above program.

Implementation of Queue using Linked List

Queues are FIFO data structures and they can be implemented by means of Linked list.

In a Queue insertion is done at the end of the Queue by means of REAR pointer. Deletion is done at the beginning of the Queue by means of FRONT pointer.

Queue representation.

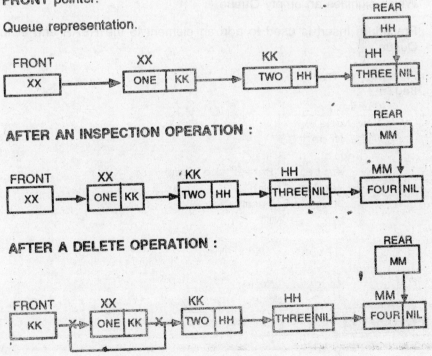

AFTER AN INSPECTION OPERATION :

AFTER A DELETE OPERATION :

The following program illustrates the basic Queue operation

Type declaration is as follows.

```
Type
      Qptr = ^Qdate;
      Qdata = Record
                  Qname : String;
                  Next : Qptr ;
              End ;
```

and the variable declaration is

```
Var
      Item,Res                  : String ;
      Front,Vptr,Rear.Node : Qptr ;
      Choice                    : integer ;
```

Initially in the main program

Front := nil ;

Which signifies an empty Queue.

Procedure Insert is used to add an element to the REAR end of the Queue.

```
Procedure Insert ;
Begin
      Clrscr;
      New(Node);
      With Node^ Do
        Begin
          Writeln('Enter the name ');
          Readln(Item) ;
          Qname := Item;
          Next := Nil ;
        End;
        If (Front = Nil) Then
         Begin
          Front := Node;
          Rear := Node ;
         End
        Else
         Begin
```

```
        Rear^.Next := Node ;
        Rear := Node ;
     End;
End;
```

When adding the first element, the Rear pointer and the Front pointer are made to point to the first node.

During the next subsequent addition, the new node is added at the Rear end of the Queue. The Rear pointer always points to the last element in the Queue.

Procedure Delete is used to delete an element from the Front end of the Queue.

```
Procedure Delete ;
Begin
     CIrscr ;
     If (Front <> Nil) then
          Begin
                Item := Front^.Qname ;
                Writeln ('Deleted item is ', Item);
                Node := Front;
                Front := Front^.Next;
                Dispose(Node);
          End
     Else
                Writeln('Queue Empty ');
End;
```

The above procedure checks the conditions for empty Queue. A temporary pointer is made to point to the first node in the Queue. The Front is made to point to the Next node in the Queue.
i.e.,

```
        Node   := Front;
        Front  : = Front^.Next;
```

Finally the memory occupied by the deleted node is returned by means of the Dispose procedure. When Front points to NIL, Queue becomes empty and further deletion cannot be performed.

The procedure View is to traverse through the FIFO structure, until

```
        Vptr^.Next := Nil
```

This procedure also checks the condition for empty Queue. Here Vptr is used to traverse through the Queue.

```pascal
Procedure View;
Begin
     Clrscr;
     Vptr :=Front;
     If (Front = Nil ) Then
          Begin
               Writeln ('Data cannot be viewed ');
               Writeln ('Empty Queue ');
          End
     Else
          Begin
               While (Vptr <> Nil ) DO
                    Begin
                       Item := Vptr^.Qname ;
                       Writeln(Item);
                       Vptr := Vptr^.Next ;
                    End;
          End;
End;
```

The Complete program is presented below.

```pascal
Program Example(Input,Output);
Uses
     Crt;
Type
     Qptr  = ^Qdata;
     Qdata = Record
             Qname : String;
             Next : Qptr ;
             End;
Var
     Item,Res : String ;
     Front,Vptr,Rear,Node : Qptr;
     Choice : Integer;
Procedure Insert;
Begin
     Clrscr;
     New(Node);
     With Node^ Do
          Begin
```

```
                    Writeln('Enter the Names ');
                    Readln(Item);
                    Qname := Item;
                    Next :=Nil;
              End;
              If (Front = Nil) Then
                  Begin
                     Front := Node;
                     Rear := Node;
                  End
               Else
                  Begin
                     Rear^.Next := Node ;
                     Rear := Node ;
                  End;
        End;

Procedure Delete ;
Begin
      CIrscr;
      If (Front <> Nil) Then
      Begin
            Item := Front^.Qname ;
            Writeln ('Deleted item is ', Item);
            Node := Front;
            Front := Front^.Next;
            Dispose(Node);
      End
Else
            Writeln('Queue Empty ');
End;

Procedure View;
Begin'
      Clrscr;
      Vptr := Front;
      If (Front = Nil) Then
          Begin
             Writeln ('Data cannot be Viewed ');
             Writeln ('Empty Queue ');
          End
      Else
          Begin                    1
```

```
While (Vptr <> Nil)Do
  Begin
     Item := Vptr^.Qname;
     Writeln(Item);
     Vptr := Vptr^.Next;
  End;
End;
End;

{Main Program Starts }

Begin
     Clrscr:
     Front :=Nil;
     Repeat
        Clrscr ;
        Writeln('Linked List Implementation of Queue ');
        Writeln('1. Insert ');
        Writeln;
        Writeln('2. Delete ');
        Writeln;
        Writeln('3. View ');
        Writeln;
        Writeln('4. Exit ');
        Writeln;
        Readln(Choice);

        Case Choice of
              1:
                 Begin
                    Clrscr;
                    Writeln('Insert Operation');
                    Insert;
                 End;
              2:
                 Begin
                    Clrscr;
                    Writeln('Delete Operation');
                    Delete;
                 End;
              3:
                 Begin
                    Clrscr;
                    Writeln('View Operation');
```

```
              View;
           End;
      4:
           Begin
              Clrscr;
              Exit;
           End;
        End;
        Writeln('Want To Continue [Y/N] ' );
        Readln(res);
     Until (Res='N');
End.
```

For output execute the above program.

Doubly Linked List

In a singly linked list we can move only in the forward direction. Doubly linked list structure allows us to traverse in both the directions.

Doubly linked list can be represented as follows :

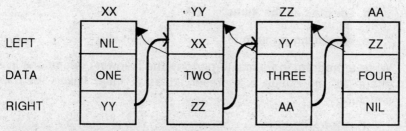

In doubly linked list each node is provided with two link fields. The left link points to the previous node and right link points to successive node in the list.

Circularly Linked List

In the circularly linked list the last node points to the first node. There is no starting and ending node. Hence the name circularly linked list.

CIRCULARLY LINKED LIST IS REPRESENTED AS

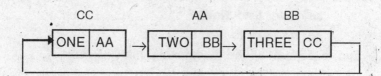

So, far we have seen some of the fundamental concepts related to pointers. It will help us to design and implementing the problem involving dynamic data structure.

Exercises

1. Define each of these terms :

    a. stack
    b. queue

2. Compare the advantages and disadvantages of implementing a stack as an array with implementing a stack as a linked list

3. Write a program in Pascal to perform the following operations in the linear linked list data structure.

    a. add an item

    b. delete an item

    c. search an item

    d. display all the items

    e. replacing an item

4. Write a program in Pascal to perform the following operations in a queue as the queue is represented as a linear linked list data structure.

    a. add an item

    b. delete an item

    c. search an item

    d. display all the items

    e. replacing an item

5. Write a program to create a linked list of nodes, each having 2 fields, .

    character field 'Name', and

    pointer field, to next node

    and to perform all the fundamental manipulations.

6. What are dynamic variables?

7. Name the standard functions in Pascal, to create and destroy dynamic variables.

Chapter - 11

GRAPHICS

In this chapter, we are focussing our attention towards the most fascinating topic of this book – Graphics. We may want to present our application program or system program in a very attractive form. Eventhough our program will do best for its purpose it requires some frills to cater to all. Moreover, pull–down and pop–up menus are quite popular nowadays. In order to do the above tasks one must know Graphics which plays a vital role in languages such as BASIC, Pascal and C.

In this chapter we will discuss some of the special features of Turbo Pascal Graphics and how it should be used to make our program a more pleasing one. Here we are considering the Turbo Pascal Version 5.5.

· Startup Procedure for Graphics

The figures and text in the graphics mode are made up of picture elements which are also called Pels or Pixels. Even in the text mode pixels are used to form the characters that appear on the screen. In Text mode we do not worry about them, because the video adapters provide built–in support for ASCII characters which are constructed by using pixels. The formation of characters, in the text mode is totally hidden to the programmers, whereas in the graphics mode the programmer has the freedom to manipulate individual pixels on the screen, to form figures and text.

Before writing a graphics program, it is essential to know the resolution of the Monitor one uses. The resolution of some of the monitors in use are given below for reference.

Graphics Driver	Graphics Mode	Mode Value	Resolution
CGA	CGAC0	0	320 * 200
	CGAC1	0	320 * 200
	CGAC2	0	320 * 200
	CGAC3	0	320 * 200
	CGAHi	0	320 * 200

Graphics Driver	Graphics Mode	Mode Value	Resolution
EGA	EGALo	0	640 * 200
	EGAHi	1	640 * 200
	EGA64Lo	0	640 * 200
	EGA64Hi	1	640 * 200
	# EGAMonoHi	3	640 * 200
	$ EGAMonoHi	3	640 * 200
HERC	HercMonoHi	0	720 * 348
VGA	VGALo	0	640 * 200
	VGAMed	1	640 * 350
	VGAHi	2	640 * 480

64 K on EGA Mono card

$ 256 K on EGA Mono card

We get very sharp images on the screen if we use monitors having higher resolution (i.e. monitors having more number of pixels).

One cannot draw figures or use graphics commands in the text mode. Before the graphics are executed, the screen must be prepared to accept the graphics commands. This is initiated by specifying the correct video driver of the system. Turbo Pascal makes this job easier by supplying video drivers which convert text mode to graphics mode. Here is a list of the video drivers (files) supported by Borland. The file names end with an extension. **BGI** which stand for Borland Graphics Interface.

Driver File Name	Video Adapters Supported
ATT.BGI	AT & T 6300 (400 line)
CGA.BGI	IBM CGA, MCGA, and compatibles
EGAVGA.BGI	IBM EGA, VGA, and compatibles

Driver File Name	Video Adapters Supported
HERC.BGI	Hercules monochrome and compatibles
IBME8514.BGI	IBM 8514 and compatibles
PC3270.BGI	IBM 3270 PC

To switch from text mode to graphics mode we use a standard procedure called '**Initgraph**'. to return to the text mode another procedure called '**Closegraph**' is used.

The general form for '**Initgraph**' is as follows.

```
Initgraph(Gd,Gm, '');
```

The procedure Initgraph takes three parameters and they are

1. the video driver to be used [Gd]

2. the graphics mode [Gm]

3. the path name to look for the video driver files.

Turbo Pascal provides another predefined constant 'detect' which automatically finds the current video driver in use and it returns an integer value. For example the statement

```
gd := detect ;
```

will store the integer value to the integer variable '**gd**' which corresponds to the graph driver in use. In this 'Initgraph' procedure, we are using another identifier '**gm**' which takes the integer value that corresponds the maximum resolution available from the monitor. Finally if the graph files are located in some other path, this may also be mentioned through this 'Initgraph' procedure. Consider the following example.

```
Uses Graph ;
Var
        Gd,Gm : Integer;
Begin
        Gd := Detect ;
        Initgraph(Gd,Gm, ' ');
        /
        /
        Closegraph ;
End.
```

Note that in the first statement we have used a standard unit provided by Turbo Pascal which contains more than 70 graphics procedures and functions. Before starting any of the graphics routine GRAPH.TPU is included – similar to using CRT when we intend to use Clrscr in the program in order to clear the screen.

Placing a Pixel in a Graphics Mode

Let us begin our graphics tour with placing a pixel in the screen. To place a pixel in a screen at particular coordinates we use the procedure Putpixel.

Syntax

```
Procedure PutPixel(X,Y : Integer; PixelColor : Word);
```

Explanation

Plots a pixel at X,Y. The color of the pixel drawn is determined by pixelColor.

Example

PutPixel(200,200,4);

Will plot a pixel at (100,100) and the color of the pixel is Red. The list of color constant is given below.

Color	Value
Black	0
Blue	1
Green	2
Cyan	3
Red	4
Magenta	5
Brown	6
LightGray	7
DarkGray	8

LightBlue	9
LightGreen	10
LightCyan	11
LightRed	12
LightMagenta	13
Yellow	14
White	15

Next we will see how to get a pixel at a particular coordinate.

The function used for this purpose is GetPixel.

Syntax

```
Function GetPixel(X,Y : Integer) : Word;
```

Explanation

Gets the color value of the pixel at X,Y.

Example

```
Color := Getpixel(50,50);
```

Will return the color value of the pixel at coordinates at (50, 50) to the identifier, color.

Drawing Figures

Turbo Pascal supports plenty of procedures to draw figures such as line, circle, arc and rectangle.

Let us examine some of the routines one by one in the following sections.

Line

Syntax

```
Procedure Line(X1,Y1,X2,Y2 : Integer);
```

Explanation

Draws a line from (x1,y1) to (x2,y2)

Example

```
Line (100,50,200,50);
```

Will draw a horizontal line from (100,50) to (200,50).

Rectangle

Syntax

```
Procedure Rectangle(x1,y1,x2,y2 : Integer);
```

Explanation

Draws a rectangle using the current line style and color.

Example

```
Rectangle (100,50,200,100);
```

Will draw a rectangle using (100,50) as x1,y1 and (200,100) as x2,y2 which resembles a box.

Bar

Syntax

```
Procedure Bar (x1,y1,x2,y2 : Integer);
```

Explanation

Draws a bar using the current fill style and color. It is nothing but a filled rectangle. The coordinates (x1,y1) define the top left corner of the bar and the coordinates (x2,y2) define the lower right corner of the bar.

Example

```
Bar (50,50,150,75);
```

Will draw a filled rectangle by using (50, 50) as the top left corner and using (150,75) as the lower right corner of the bar.

Bar3d

Syntax

```
Procedure Bar3D(x1,y1, x2,y2    : Integer ;
                        Depth : Word;
                        Top   : Boolean);
```

Explanation

By using the current fill style and color the procedure draws a three dimensional cube. The coordinates (x1,y1) and (x2,y2) define the upper left and lower right positions of the cube. Here the parameter depth specifies the depth of the cube, in terms of pixels. If the boolean identifier Top is true (i.e. Topon), then the cube has a top with the same fill pattern and color as the face. There would not be a top if the boolean identifier is set to false (i.e. Topoff).

Example

```
Bar3d(50,50,150,75,20,Topon);
```

Will draw a 3d cube by using the coordinates (50,50) and (150,75) as the upper left and lower right position of the cube. The depth of the cube is 20 and the cube has a top with the same fill pattern and color, as the boolean identifier is set to True.

Circle

Syntax

```
Procedure Circle (X,Y: integer ;
              Radius : Word);
```

Explanation

Draws a circle using (X,Y) as the centre point.

Example

```
        Circle (320,100,50);
```

Will draw a circle of radius 50 using (320,100) as centre point.

Arc

Syntax

```
        Procedure Arc (X,Y : Integer  ; StAngle,
                    EndAngle, Radius : Word);
```

Explanation

Draws a circular arc from start angle to end angle, using (x, y) as the centre point.

Example

```
Arc (320,100,0,180,50);
```
Will draw a circular arc from start angle(0) to end angle(180), using (320,100) as the centre point and taking radius as 50.

Pieslice

Syntax

```
Procedure PieSlice (X,Y : Integer: StAngle,
                         EndAngle,Radius : word);
```

Explanation

Draws and fills a pie slice, using (X,Y) as the centre point, and drawing from start angle to end angle.

Example

```
        PieSlice(100,100,0,180,50);
```

Will draw filled semicircle of radius 50 and taking (100,100) as centre point from starting angle 0 to ending angle 180.

Ellipse

Syntax

```
Procedure   Ellipse(X,Y       : integer;
            StAngle, EndAngle  : Word;
            XRadius, YRadius   : Word);
```

Explanation

Draws an elliptical arc from start angle to end angle, using (X,Y) as the centre point.

Example

```
Ellipse (320,100,0,360,50,25);
```

Will draw an elliptical arc from start angle(0) to end angle(360),using (320,100) as the centre point and taking 50 as Xradius and 25 as Yradius.

Floodfill

Syntax

```
Procedure FloodFill (X,Y : Integer;
        Border : Word);
```

Explanation

Fills a bounded region with the current fill pattern and color.

Example

```
Circle (100,100,20);
FloodFill(100,100, GetMaxColor);
```

In this case we will get a circle of radius 20, with (100,100) as the centre point. Here the floodfill is used to fill the circle and the color is the maximum color available by the system. For example CGA monitors supports 16 colors. It is different for VGA and EGA type of monitors.

Printing Text Message in a Graphics Mode

Now let us demonstrate how a text message can be displayed in a graphics mode. To print text message the conventional procedure Write or Writeln can not be used. In graphics mode we use Outtext and Outtextxy to display the text message. The usage of the above procedures is given below.

```
OutText(TextString);
```

and

```
OutTextXY(X,Y,TextString);
```

Where X,Y are Integer

The above two procedures send a string to the output device. The only difference is that latter displays the text string in the specified location given as X,Y.

In graphics mode we are considering the positions in terms of pixels rather than row and column as in gotoxy.

Here is a program to demonstrate the above two procedures.

```
Program Example;
Uses Graph;
Var
    Gd,Gm : Integer;
Begin
    Gd : = Detect ;
    Initgraph(Gd,Gm,'');
```

```
Outtext('Welcome To Turbo Pascal Graphics ');
Outtextxy(300, 50, 'Welcome To Turbo Pascal Graphics');
Readln;
End.
```

In the above program, the procedure outtext will display the message 'Welcome To Turbo Pascal Graphics' in the upper left corner whereas the second procedure Outtextxy will display the same message in the position (300,50) given as x and y.

The above two routines Outtext( ) and Outtextxy( ) will display the message in normal mode. The letters formed through this mode is also not so pleasing. Turbo Pascal provides some graphic character (fonts) handling files which enhance the output text in a more attractive way. The Font files will have an extension name as .CHR. The list of font files that are supported by Turbo Pascal along with their constant value is given below. To specify a particular font in a program we can give its corresponding value instead of the font name.

Font File	Font Provided	Value
GOTH.CHR	Stroked Gothic	4
LITT.CHR	Stroked Small Character	2
SANS.CHR	Stroked Sansserif	3
TRIPS.CHR	Stroked Triplex	1

In addition to the above, Turbo Pascal also supports the default font which will have 0 as the constant value.

The procedure related to handle these font files is Settextstyle which expects three parameters. The general form is given below.

```
Procedure SetTextStyle(Font,
            Direction: Wrod;
            Charsize : Word);
```
Where

Font is the font file name or the constant value or any one of the file mentioned above.

Direction is the number either 0 or 1 which makes the output to display in Horizontal direction or in Vertical direction.

The constant value for Horizontal direction and Vertical direction is given below.

Direction	Value
HorizDir	0
VertDir	1

The third parameter to the procedure SettextStyle is the character size or magnification factor and it also varies from 1 to 10

Here is an example to call the above procedure

```
SetTexStyle(triplexfont,Horizdir,4);
Outtextxy(50,10, 'Turbo pascal' );
```

The above call will display the message 'Turbo Pascal' in Horizontal direction by using a triplex font file and character magnification size in 4

Here is an Example program which involves all the four font files.

```
Program Example (Input,Output);
Uses graph;
Var
    Gd,Gm : Integer;
Begin
    Gd :=Detect;
    Initgraph(Gd,Gm, '');

    SetTextStyle(Smallfont,Horizdir,5);
    Outtextxy (25,10, 'Turbo Pascal in Small font' );

    SetTextStyle(Gothicfont,Horizdir,5);
    Outtextxy (25,20, 'Turbo Pascal in Gothic font' );
    SetTextStyle(Sansseriffont,Horizdir,5);
    Outtextxy (25,60, 'Turbo Pascal in Sansserif font' );

    SetTextStyle(Triplexfont,Horizdir,5);
    Outtextxy (25,100, 'Turbo Pascal in Triplex font' );

    SetTextStyle(Defaultfont,Horizdir,5);
    Outtextxy (25,150, 'Turbo Pascal in Default font' );

    Readln;
    Closegraph;
End.
```

Output

Turbo Pascal in Small font

Turbo Pascal in gothic font

Turbo Pascal in Sansserif font

Turbo Pascal in Triplex font

Turbo Pascal in default font

As most of the programs in this chapter are screen oriented, execute the program to get a clear idea.

So far, we have seen some of the graphic functions and procedures which make our programming life a little more intresting.

Programming is an art and it is more so especially in graphics programming. The graph unit supports more than 70 routines in Turbo Pascal Ver 5.5 and still more in version 6.0. It is impossible to brows all the routines available in the graph unit. The purpose of this chapter is to induce an interest in Graphics. So, the rest of this topic is left to the programmers who wish to improve their skills in the art of programming.

SOLVED PROBLEMS

1. Program to print Olympic circle.

Program Example (Input, Output);

```
Uses crt, graph;
Var
Gd, gm: integer;
Begin
  Initgraph (gd, gm,' ');
  Gd: = detect;
  Settextstyle (triplexfont, horizdir,4)
  Outtextxy (200,0, 'Olympic 1996');
  Settextstyle (triplexfont, horizdir, 2);
  Outtextxy (250, 35, 'at atlanta');
  Circle (150,100,100);
  Circle (300,100,100)
  Circle (450,100,100);
  Circle (225,145,100);
  Circle (375,145,100);
Readln
End.
```

Output

Olympic 1996
at atlanta

2. Program to print Doordarshan symbol.
{ Program written by using CGA monitor
Make appropriate changes for other monitors }

Program Example (Input, Output);

```
Uses graph;
Var
   Gd,gm:integer;
Begin
   Gd:=detect;
   Initgraph (gd, gm,'');
   Circle (305,100,70)
   Settextstyle (Gothicfont, Horizdir, 5);
   Outextxy (275,75, 'DD');
   Arc (320,100,0,180,200);
   Arc (350,100,0,180,170);
   Arc (150,100,180,360,30);
   Arc (290,100,180,360,200);
   Arc (260,100,180,360,170);
```

```
         Arc (460,100,0,180,30);
         Readln;
         Closegraph;
     End
```

Output

CHAPTER -12

AN INTRODUCTION TO
OBJECT ORIENTED PROGRAMMING

Revolution takes place not only in history, but also in the evolution of programming languages as is the case with OOP– the hottest topic the field of programming languages have ever seen. In this chapter, let us introduce some of the paradigm of object oriented programming and see, as to what makes us to deviate from conventional ways of coding to the modern trend.

Languages such as BASIC, C, FORTRAN and Pascal (earlier Versions) are called Procedural languages. The statements in these languages are coded to perform certain specific tasks such as to get input from the user, doing some calculation and output the result. For smaller tasks, such as the one mentioned above these procedural languages work fine without much difficulty.

When the program becomes a little bit complex we use the principle of dividing a program into smaller pieces which is otherwise called a procedure or a function. It also makes our program into, a more structured one.

As programs grow larger and more complex, the languages so far seen (even structured programming languages) find it difficult to manage and OOP comes into rescue, and solves the problem.

The main reason for a switch from procedural language to object oriented language is, the way they treat the data. In a procedural language program gets precedence over the data, i.e., data is given a second class status, whereas in the object oriented programs data plays a vital role. In addition, code and data are considered as equal partners.

The history of OOP dates back to 1960 when research started through Simula programming language. The real credit goes to Smalltalk– the first successful and complete object oriented programming language developed at Xerox corporation's PARC (Palo Alto Research Centre), which took nearly 10 years to complete. Today more than 100 languages support OOP features which indicates that a language can not withstand in the field of programming languages if it lacks the OOP feature.

Let us now consider the OOP features through Turbo Pascal. It is a blend of the best features taken from Apple's Object Pascal and AT & T's C++ Programming language. Thus Turbo Pascal Version 5.5 paves a way to this exciting feature and in version 6.0 it is further refined to a more spectacular way.

Syntax for object class

The term Object is nothing but an extension of record. In record, we declare only the members (fields), whereas in an object, in addition to the member declaration, we also declare procedures and functions used in the program. The member declaration in an object is called 'Instance variables'. The functions and procedures in an object are called 'Methods'. Combining all the above into a single object class is called encapsulation.

The syntax for the object class is as follows :

```
Type
Class name ; Object
        Field declaration;
        /
        method declaration;
end;
```

Here the object, class name, is the object class identifier and the naming of class follow the same rules as that for any identifier. The field declaration is member declaration and method declaration is procedure or function declaration.

The object class is defined similar to a record. The field declaration in an object is similar to field declaration in a record.

Next we will see how methods (procedures and functions) are declared inside an Object.

The general form for the procedure declaration inside an object is

```
procedure object class.method name(Variable list);
Begin
        Statement;
        /
        Statement;
End;
```

Here the object class is the object class name and method name is nothing but a particular procedure (method) name. It is followed by variable list to be passed to the procedure.

The general form of the function declaration inside an object is

```
Function object class.method name(Var.list): Data type;
          Begin
          Statement;
          /
          Statement;
End;
```

Here the object class is the object class name and method name is nothing but a particular function (method) name. It is followed by a variable list to be passed to the functions. Since it is a function it returns only one value to the main. The data type returned by such a function should also be given in the function declaration itself.

Before an object could be used, it should be declared in the Var section as a record type declared as a record variable. The declaration takes the following form

Var

```
Object Name : Object Class;
```

Here object name is an identifier which we are going to use in the main program and the object class is the one which we have already declared as an object in the type declaration itself.

Consider the following object declaration.

```
Type
        Stdrec = Object
                    StdName : String;
                    StdNo : Integer;
                    Tam,Eng,Mat : Integer;
                    Procedure GetInput;
                    Procedure DisOutput;
                 End;
```

In the above object declaration StdName,StdNo,Tam,Eng, and Mat are called as Instance variables. The procedures GetInput and DispOutput are called Methods.

Now consider the following program which uses the above object.

```
Program Example (Input,Output);
Uses Crt;
Type
```

```
Stdrec = Object
                StdName : String;
                StdNo : Integer;
                Tam,Eng,Mat : Integer;
                Procedure GetInput;
                Procedure DisOutput;
            End;

Procedure Stdrec.GetInput;
Begin
    Clrscr;
    Writeln ('Enter Student Name ');
    Readln (StdName);
    Writeln('Enter ExamNo ');
    Readln(StdNo);
    Writeln('Enter Tam,Eng,Mat Marks ');
    Readln(Tam,Eng,Mat);
End;

Procedure Stdrec.DisOutput;
Var
    Tot : Integer;
Begin
    Writeln ('Name of The Student : ',StdName);
    Writeln (' Exam No : ',StdNo);
    Tot := Tam + Eng + Mat ;
    Writeln (' Total Marks : ', Tot);
End;
Var
    Markrec : Stdrec ;
Begin
    Markrec.GetInput;
    Markrec.DisOutput;
    Readln;
End.
```

Output

Enter Student Name
Rajesh
Enter ExamNo
202
Enter Tam, Eng, Mat Marks

67 78 91

Name of The Student: Rajesh
Exam No : 202
Total marks : 236

The program starts by calling the method GetInput of markrec. In this method user has to give name, stdno and marks for the three subjects. Then the method Dispoutput of markrec is called. In this method the marks are added and it is displayed along with the name and exam no.

The above program is a very good example to illustrate the concept of encapsulation which is considered as one of the important properties of the object oriented programming.

Now, we will see another important property of OOP – **Inheritance.**

Inheritance

If a child resembles in some of the characteristics of his/her parent, say for example, in appearance or behaviour, we say that the child has inherited the characteristics of his/her parent. Similarly in OOP, for example, if we have an object A and we want to declare two more objects by name B and C which contain some of the instance variables and methods that are present in the object A, then instead of declaring individual objects it is enough that we declare the first object which contains the common fields of both the objects and then the fields pertaining to object B and C alone, thus by making use of the property – Inheritance. Here we call the object A as the parent class. The objects B and C are called as subclasses.

Defining on object subclass

Here is the general form for defining an object subclass.

```
type
     Classname = object (parent class)
               field declaration ;
               /
               field declaration ;

               method declaration ;
               /
               method declaration ;
          end;
```

Here class name is the new object subclass's identifier and parent class is the name of the subclass's parent class. The field declaration and method declaration are usual declarations found in the object.

Further, consider the following two objects – the latter one being inherited from the former.

```
Type

    Stdrec = Object
                    Stdname : string ;
                    ExamNo : Integer ;
                    Procedure Init;
                    Procedure GetName;
                    Procedure GetExamNo;
            End;

    Result = Object (Stdrec)
                    TotMarks : Integer:
                    Procedure GetMarks ;
                    Procedure Class;
            End;
```

In the above declaration we have stdrec as a parent object and the purpose of this object is, to receive Name and ExamNo for the student record. Also we have another object Result, which has inherited two fields such as Name and Examno from the Object Stdrec. Here the instance variables and methods available to the subclass (Result) are a superset of the parent class's(Stdrec) instance variables and methods.

Now let us consider the complete program to demonstrate the above concept.

```
Program Example(Input,Output);
Uses Crt;
Type
    Stdrec = Object
                    Stdname : string ;
                    ExamNo : Integer ;
                    Procedure Init;
                    Procedure GetName;
                    Procedure GetExamNo;
            End;


    Result = Object (Stdrec)
                    TotMarks : Integer ;
                    Procedure GetMarks ;
```

```
                Procedure Class;
            End;

Procedure Stdrec.Init;
    Begin
            StdName : = ' ';
            ExamNo  : = 0;
    End;

    Procedure Stdrec.GetName;
    Begin
        Writeln('Enter Name ');
        Readln(StdName);
    End;

    Procedure Stdrec.GetExamNo;
    Begin
        Writeln('Enter ExamNo ');
        Readln(ExamNo);
    End;

    Procedure Result.GetMarks;
    Begin
        Writeln('Enter Marks ');
        Readln(TotMarks);
    End;

    Procedure Result.Class;
    Var
        C : String;
    Begin
        If TotMarks < 300 Then
            C := 'Second '
        Else
            C := 'First';
        Writeln(' Name : ', StdName);
        Writeln(' No : ', ExamNo);
        Writeln(' Marks : ', TotMarks);
        Writeln(' Class : ', C);
    End;
Var
    Resultobj : Result ;
Begin
```

```
      Clrscr;
      ResultObj. Init;
      ResultObj. GetName;
      ResultObj. GetExamNo;
      ResultObj. GetMarks;
      ResultObj. Class;
End.
```

Output.

Enter Name
Lavan
Enter ExamNo
1001
Enter Marks
450
Name : Lavan
No : 1001
Marks : 450
Class ; First

Enter Name
Kusan
Enter ExamNo
1002
Enter Marks
250

Name : Kusan
No : 1002
Marks ; 250
Class : Second

First of all note that in the variable declaration of the main we have declared ResultObj of the type Result. The object stdrec is used as a parent class to the subclass of Result.

Now let us discuss yet another important feature of OOP – **Polymorphism.**

In the previous section we saw that a subclass can inherit some of the instance variables and methods of the parent class, in addition to its own instance variables and methods. While inheriting some of the methods from the parent class, we also have a choice to modify the methods of the parent class. Polymorphism provides the ability of doing so. Thus it is considered as the most powerful tool of object oriented programming.

As polymorphic methods are called virtual methods, the method which we want to modify should be appended with the keyword virtual both in the parent class and in the subclass. Also note that once if the method has been declared as virtual, it must remain as virtual in the following subclasses.

Here we introduce a new term – Constructor. A constructor is nothing but a special procedure. We use the keyword constructor instead of procedure, so as to perform internal manipulations to enable the use of virtual methods in an object class.

The following is the syntax diagram to define a Turbo Pascal polymorphic subclass.

```
Type
    Class name = Object (Parent class)
                    field declarations ;
                    constructor declarations;
                    method declarations ; virtual;
            End;
```

Here the constructor declaration is nothing but an object class declaration. The method declaration which is appended with a keyword Virtual is the prototype of function or procedure.

From the above declaration it is evident that it is neccessary to invoke the constructor first before calling any of the other methods. The system will crash if we are not doing so.

Here is an example declaration which is to be used as a part of the subsequent problem.

```
Type
    Stdrec = Object
                StdName : String;
                ExamNo  : Integer;
                Constructor Init;
                Procedure GetName;
                Procedure GetExamNo;
                Procedure Display ; virtual ;
            End;
```

```
Result = Object (Stdrec)
          TotMarks : Integer ;
          Constructor Init;
          Procedure GetMarks;
          Procedure Display ; Virtual
          End;
```

The next task before us is to know how we can call an inherited virtual method.

Here is a syntax diagram to solve the above problem.

```
Parent class.methodname(argument.list);
```

The following example method will clearly make the task of our understanding very easy.

```
Procedure stdrec.Display;
    Begin
        Writeln(' Name : ', StdName);
        Writeln('No : ', ExamNo);
    End;

    Procedure Result.Display ;
        Begin
          Stdrec.Display;
          Writeln('Marks : ', TotMarks);
        End;
```

In the above procedure, within the procedure Result.Display we call the method display, by preceding method name with the parent class'name and a period(.).

Here is a complete program to demonstrate the concept of polymorphism.

```
Program Example (Input,Output);
Uses Crt;
Type
    Stdrec = Object
          StdName : String;
          ExamNo : Integer;
          Constructor Init;
          Procedure GetName;
```

```
        Procedure GetExamNo;
        Procedure Display ; Virtual ;
        End;


    Result = Object (Stdrec)
            TotMarks : Integer ;
            Constructor Init;
            Procedure GetMarks;
            Procedure Display ; Virtual;
        End;

Constructor Stdrec.Init;
Begin
        StdName := ' ';
        ExamNo := 0;
    End;

    Procedure Stdrec.GetName;
    Begin
        Writeln('Enter Name ');
        Readln(StdName);
    End;

    Procedure Stdrec.GetExamNo;
    Begin
        Writeln('Enter ExamNo ');
        Readln(ExamNo);
    End;

    Procedure Stdrec.Display;
    Begin
        Writeln(' Name : ', StdName );
        Writeln(' No : ', ExamNo);
    End;
    Constructor Result.Init;
    Begin
        Stdrec.Init:
        Totmarks := 0 ;
    End;
    Procedure Result.GetMarks;
    Begin
        Writeln('Enter Marks ');
```

```
            Readln(TotMarks);
      End;

      Procedure Result.Display ;
      Var
            C :  String ;
      Begin
            if TotMarks <300 Then
                  C := 'Second '
            Else
                  C := 'First' ;
                  Stdrec.Display;
            Writeln('Marks :', TotMarks);
            Writeln('Class : ',C);
      End;
Var
            ResultObj : Result;
Begin
            Clrscr;
            ResultObj.Init;
            ResultObj.GetName;
            ResultObj.GetExamNo;
            ResultObj.GetMarks;
            ResultObj.Display;
            Readln;
End.
```

Output.

Enter Name
Seetha
Enter ExamNo
1001
Enter Marks
678
Name : Seetha
No : 1001
Marks : 678
Class : First

Final thought : Though the example programs that we have
encountered so far seem to be very easy, the real world of OOP is
anything but simple. There are many features which make the language

to support OOP, here we have seen only some of the important features of the OOP. The object of this chapter is to make our voyage to OOP a comfortable one. The remaining features are left to the court of programmers who are considered as best judges for analysing the pros and cons of the language.

APPENDIX – A

RESERVED WORDS

The following words are reserved in Turbo Pascal. They may not be redefined by the program.

absolute	external	nil	shl
and	file	not	shr
array	forward	overlay	string
begin	for	of	then
case	function	or	type
const	goto	packed	to
div	inline	procedure	until
do	if	program	var
downto	in	record	while
else	lable	repeat	with
end	mod	set	xor

APPENDIX – B

PREDEFINED IDENTIFIERS.

The following identifiers are predefined and meant for specific purposes. If we redefine these identifiers, we may lose the original feature. It is better to leave as it is.

Addr	Darkgray	HiResColor	Mode
Append	Delline	IOresult	Mkdir
ArcTan	Delay	Input	MsDos
Assign	Delete	Insline	New
Aux	Draw	Insert	NormVideo
AuxInPtr	Dseg	Int	
AuxOutPtr		Integer	Odd
	EOF	Intr	Ofs
Black	EOLN		Ord
BlockRead	Erase	kbd	Output
BlockWrite	Execute	keyPressed	Ovrpath
Blue	Exit		
Boolean	Exp	Length	Palette
Brown		LightBlue	Pi
Buflen	False	LightCyan	Plot
Byte	Filepos	LightGray	Port
	Fileszie	LightGreen	PortW
Chain	Fillchar	LightMagenta	pos
Char	Flush	LightRed	Pred
Chdir	Frac	Ln	Ptr
Chr		Lo	
Close	GetDir	LongFilePos	Random
ClrEol	GetMem	LongFileSeek	Randomize
Clrscr	GotoXY	LongSeek	Read
Con	GraphBack-	LowVideo	Readln
ConInPtr	ground	Lst	Real
ConOutPtr	GraphColor	LstOutptr	Rmdir
Concat	Graphmode		Round
ConstPtr	GraphWindow	Move	Red
Copy	Green	Magenta	Release
Cos		MaxInt	Rename
CrtExit	Halt	Mark	Reset
CrtInit	HeapPtr	Mem	ReWrite
CSeg	Hi	MemW	
Cyan	Hires	Memavail	Seek

SeekEof	Swap	Trunc	WhereY
seekEoln		UpCase	White
Sin	Text	Usr	Write
Sizeof	TextBack	UsrInPtr	Writeln
Sqr	ground	UserOutPtr	
Sqrt	TextColor		Yellow
Str	Textmode	Val	
SSet	Trm		
Succ	True	WhereX	

BIBLIOGRAPHY

Byron S. Gottfried, Schaum's Outline Series, Theory and Problems of Programming with PASCAL,McGraw Hill Book Company, 1987

Bjarne stroustrupp; What is "Object Oriented Programming"? (1991 revised edition); AT & T Bell Laboratory ; Murrary Hill, New Jersey 07974

Mark Goodwin, Teach Yourself Pascal, Advanced Computer Books (MIS Press), 1990

Michael Schneider, G., Steven C Bruell, Advanced Programming and Problem Solving with Pascal, John Wiley & Sons, 1987

Murat M.Tanik, Kyle Townsend, Winston Cheng and Stephen L.Stepoway, Graphics Programming with Turbo Pascal, Learners Press, 1992

Paul L. Schlieve, Illustrated Turbo Pascal 5.5, BPB, 1990

Radha Ganesan P.Srinivasan N,C in 10 Hours, Galgotia Publications Pvt ltd, 1993

Robert Lafore, Object Oriented Programming in Microsoft C++, Galgotia Publications Pvt Ltd. 1993

Scott D.Palmer, Mastering Turbo Pascal 6, BPB,1991

Tom Swan, Mastering Turbo Pascal, BPB, 1987

INDEX